slow motion

JENNIFER DUPREE

P.O. Box 10
Yarmouth, Maine 04096
www.islandportpress.com
info@islandportpress.com

The stories in this book reflect the author's recollection of events. Some names and details have been altered for privacy.

First Edition: 2026
Printed in the United States of America

ISBN: 978-1-952143-46-5
Library of Congress Control Number: 2025941179

Cover and interior design by Katrina Noble
Cover image: *Oleanders*, By Vincent van Gogh, c. 1888. Oil on canvas. The Metropolitan Museum of Art, New York. Source: Metmuseum.org. Public Domain.

PRAISE FOR *Slow Motion*

"I've never read a friendship story like this one. Dupree writes with mordant humor, grand affection, and righteous rage in nearly equal amounts, giving us a vivid picture of what it means to both friends—the sanguine, wry, severely disabled Marcel and the emotionally messy, able-bodied Jen—to be accepted for exactly who they are. I felt not so much inspired by this story as welcomed into it." —Monica Wood, national bestselling author of *How to Read a Book*

"*Slow Motion* is an emotionally rich tale of self-empowerment and hard-won advocacy in the face of a disgraceful system that limits and endangers the lives of people with disabilities. This powerful story needs to be told, and Dupree does so by embracing the humanity and humor shared by two people who genuinely care for each other."—Marianne Leone, author of *Jesse: A Mother's Story*

"*Slow Motion* is not a story about disabilities—it's a gorgeously rendered love letter to a dear friend. With a lyrical touch and searing honesty, Dupree allows us to fall in love over and over again with two people who need each other in that old human way. This book, these sentences, this friendship are shockingly stunning."—Dave Patterson, author of *Soon the Light Will Be Perfect* and *Euphoria*

"I came to this book because of its focus on disability. What will most stick with me is its depiction of friendship. This is a startlingly tender—and often hilarious—book by a razor-sharp writer. Dupree weaves in the history of cerebral palsy without falling into didacticism; she sketches lively portraits of her friendship with Marcel without bogging down the narrative. Every scene shines."—Jeremy Klemin, writer and disability advocate

ALSO BY JENNIFER DUPREE

What Do You Want From Me?
The Miraculous Flight of Owen Leach

OTHER MEMOIRS FROM ISLANDPORT PRESS

Moon in Full
Marpheen Chann

The Ghosts of Walter Crockett
W. Edward Crockett

Always Game
Christi Elliott

And Poison Fell From the Sky
MarieThérèse Martin

We're Going Home
Cynthia Thayer

For you, Marcel. No one has ever been a better friend.

CONTENTS

Author's Note 9

You've Got a Friend 11

How To 25

Speculation 35

We Are Family 45

(Re)create 59

Joe 79

Photographic Evidence 85

These Things Happen 95

Care and Keeping 105

Do Not Resuscitate 125

Let's (Not) Talk About Sex 131

Home Sweet Home 141

(Im)personal Care 157

Your Call Is Important to Us 169

When You Die 181

You Say It's Your Birthday 189

Epilogue 201

Sources 203

About the Author 205

Acknowledgments 206

AUTHOR'S NOTE

I began writing this book as both a way to document the life experiences Marcel and I have had, but also as a tribute to the way Marcel offers his friendship to me.

For much of the book, I relay events and emotions to you, dear reader. But there are places where the emotion, the circumstance, or both, feel intimate enough that I can only relay them directly to Marcel. And so, in those places, you'll note the use of the second person, the "you" on the page.

This second person, the "you," implicates the reader in the intimacy of the moment. That is, the reader becomes part of the story. Sometimes this feels slightly off or uncomfortable, and that's intentional. Sometimes living with a disability in an able-bodied world is uncomfortable. Other times, the "you" feels like a whispered secret, the unveiling of something private. And that's right, too.

And, yes, I am an able-bodied person, telling the story of friendship in which one of us is disabled. I'm so glad I get to tell this story—that Marcel wants me to tell this story—but this memoir is by no means a full stop. There are many disabled voices—many disabled stories—out there and I believe we—writers, publishers, and readers—need to create space for those voices. We have to demand that those voices be heard.

I wrote this book for you, dear reader, to share with you what I have seen and experienced in our ableist culture. It's my hope that, through reading it, you'll find ways to be an ally in the quest for inclusivity. But first and foremost, I wrote this book for you, Marcel. To thank you for shaping me into the kind of friend I am.

You’ve Got a Friend

Now, ain’t it good to know that you’ve got a friend
When people can be so cold?

—Carole King, *You’ve Got a Friend*

Marcel and I were on the sidewalk in a hospital parking lot. It was April 2022, and he’d been in the hospital since right before Christmas. The hospital nurses, whom he has come to love and who regularly text me Snapchat photos they take with him when I’m not there, got him up and into his fully motorized wheelchair. He doesn’t have clothes other than the unlaundered ones he arrived at the hospital in, so they wrapped a sheet and blanket around his hospital gown. A few weeks ago, I went to the group home to get his sneakers, because he wanted to get out of bed and into his wheelchair and the hospital wanted him to have something on his feet. The group home staff—all new since his hospitalization—couldn’t find his sneakers. If I hadn’t been so flabbergasted—*how could they lose his sneakers?*—I might have thought to get him some clothes, too. I bought him new sneakers and forgot about clothes until this moment. Next time I go, which will be later in the week, I’ll stop and gather a bag of sweatpants, sweatshirts, socks, and t-shirts. For now, though, he had to wear the gown and sheet.

At this point, he was medically better, but the group home where he'd lived for the past three years was refusing to take him back because they say he requires more care than they can provide. Marcel is seventy-two, and he's lived with cerebral palsy his entire life, the complications from which are compounding as he ages. He and I disagree with the group home about how much care he requires and what they are contractually obligated to provide. His lawyer from Disability Rights Maine, whom I contacted with his permission when the group home nurse manager stated that Marcel would be "better suited" to a nursing home, also disagrees with the group home. For weeks, we've been in meetings with doctors, nurses, social workers, group home staff, his lawyer, and the group home's lawyer. At this point, we were both exhausted and afraid he might lose this fight and have to return to the nursing home: Marcel lived in this nursing home—a place that offers almost no freedom and very little financial autonomy and where he had no peers and no opportunities to meet any—for nearly twenty years. Now that he's in his seventies, he would be closer in age to many of the people in the nursing home, but he has none of the cognitive decline common with that population. This day, though, was bright and mild, and Marcel wanted to get outside.

I walked beside him and chatted, and when we came to a big puddle in the middle of the sidewalk, I said we should turn around. But Marcel shook his head and pointed his face in the direction we were going. He seemed to know the puddle was just a puddle, shallow and nothing to worry about, so I followed him as he rolled forward.

It was not just a puddle. It was a giant crater in the asphalt, the gravel soft from rain. His front wheels went in and he pitched too far forward to be able to back up his heavy chair. He wasn't in danger of tipping, but he was well and truly stuck. I felt pretty sure I was going to have a panic attack because I'd been having them, and this seemed like a reasonable time to have one. Panic attacks were a fairly new addition to my life, and I both hated them and was deeply ashamed of them. Despite what my therapist said, they felt like failure. But, even with Marcel stuck in a hole, and even though I was nervous, the panic didn't come. Maybe because I was with him and my body knew I needed to keep it together.

Dryly, I said, "Well. This is bad."

And, just as I'd hoped, Marcel laughed.

I tried to yank the chair back by its handles, but it weighs a couple hundred pounds and there was just no way I could make it budge. I needed help.

There was no one in the parking lot, and it was a good distance back to the hospital. I couldn't just leave Marcel pitched forward into a hole because, while it didn't seem likely, he might topple and land on his face.

Just as I was about to call up to the nurses' station to have someone come out and rescue us, security came by and asked if we needed help. With me pushing and the security guy pulling, we freed the chair. Marcel and I thanked him and headed back inside, the hospital's white sheet and blanket now tracked with muddy wheel-prints.

On the way back inside, I began trembling, which was the way my body had been responding during and after panic attacks. I was not well, or not as well as I wanted to be, and yet I was proud of myself for holding it together to help Marcel. In that moment, I felt better than I had in weeks.

The first panic attack I had was while driving on the Maine Turnpike. Early in December 2021, I was going down to New Hampshire to meet a friend for breakfast and I started shaking like I was freezing. I cranked the heat and I was still shaking and my heart was wild and then I was suddenly convinced my car was about to fall apart. It feels important for me to remember that the panic came before the certainty there was something wrong with my car so that I could better make sense of what was happening. I pulled into the rest stop at Kennebunk, left the car running, and got out to look under it. I am not a car person. I've never even put air in my tires, so I don't know what I was looking for. I didn't have a flat tire, at least.

I went into the rest stop, peed, washed my hands, smoothed the frizz out of my hair. *I'm fine,* I told myself. *The car is fine.* Before I headed back out, I called my husband and asked him if my car was due for service. Steve said no, it just went in and everything was fine. "Why?" he asked. "No reason," I lied.

I made it to breakfast, although by the time I got there, I'd been shaking so much and for so long that my body hurt. I said nothing about it to my friend.

I ate my pancake and drank my iced coffee and my legs trembled the whole time, but I smiled and kept up my side of the conversation. The restaurant was crowded and delightfully overdecorated and it's one of my favorite places, and my friend is one of my favorite friends, but on this day, I couldn't enjoy any of it. To explain my shaking, I might have said something like, "It's cold in here." My friend is a warm, loving, and perceptive person and I felt like I'd gotten away with something when she didn't ask what was wrong with me.

When it was time to leave, I waited for my friend to drive away and then I sat in my car and cried because I honestly didn't think I could make myself drive home and I didn't understand what was going on with me. I was forty-six, and while I'd suffered with depression and anxiety for as long as I could remember, nothing like this had ever happened to me. It would be months before I went to the doctor and told her I thought I was having panic attacks, and she asked if I'd ever been depressed and I started to cry. She'd tell me, gently, that sometimes panic attacks follow depression. But now, all I knew was something was wrong. I wouldn't call Steve and ask him to drive an hour and a half to come get me, because he's so nice he would.

I drove no more than forty miles an hour all the way home because the faster I went, the harder I panicked. I called Steve when I was halfway home and told him I was just leaving so that he wouldn't notice how long it took me to get home. I didn't want to worry him.

I only agreed to therapy so I could stop taking my anti-anxiety medication. In my family, medication means weakness, and weakness means you've failed. I realize I'm a grown woman, but I have never been able to stop wanting to not disappoint my parents.

I liked Dr. G right away. He's fatherly and soft-spoken and, at my first visit, the book *Being Mortal* was tented open on his desk, which made me like him even more because he's a reader and also because, even though I'm a librarian and I shouldn't, I judge what people read and this is the type of book nice people read.

We talked about my childhood, my marriage, my work. Over the course of many sessions, I told him about my friendship with Marcel. I never know exactly how to talk about Marcel, especially in therapy, because I worry the therapist will point to my "nurturing" him and suggest some latent unfulfilled mothering desires (it's happened). And when Steve and I talk about Marcel to new acquaintances, it's usually met with them telling us how lucky he is to have us and then us saying we're lucky to have him, and, frankly, the whole thing feels a bit like a dog-and-pony show. But after I confessed that I'd been thinking about ways to die, Dr. G wanted to know what was anchoring me to life and, because I was trying to be honest, I told him Marcel was at the top of the list.

Marcel and I have been friends since 1997, when I was twenty-two and less than a year into my first "real" job as Activity Director in a large nursing facility in Lewiston, Maine. Marcel, who was forty-six, became a resident after it was no longer possible for him to live on his own. Marcel was, at the time of his nursing home admission, younger than I am as I write this. He was thirty or forty or fifty years younger than almost every other nursing home resident. And while he had similar mobility issues and care needs related to activities of daily living (bathing, dressing, eating, toileting) that other residents had, he had no confusion, no forgetfulness, and no trouble understanding everything that happened to him and around him. I got to know him in the way I got to know all the residents—by asking what he liked to do and then inviting him to programs that might be of interest—music, Catholic Mass, Bingo. I liked his sense of humor, his curiosity, his kindness, but I didn't really get to know him until he asked me to help him learn to read.

I told Dr. G that Marcel has cerebral palsy and we'd been friends for twenty-four years and that I'm his person—the person who goes to medical appointments with him and stays with him for hours if he's in the hospital and takes him Christmas shopping and registers him for Pine Tree Camp and calls tech support when his communication device goes on the fritz. I'm the person who knows he's allergic to Reglan and that he takes his coffee with five creams and five sugars and the fact that he loves dogs but hates the smell of farm animals, mostly because he can't use his hands to block his nose to mitigate the smell. I told him I'm sure Marcel could go on without me, but that it would be harder and that, no matter how much I'd like to take an early exit, I can't justify making his life harder.

Dr. G sat casually in his desk chair, legs crossed, arms resting on the arm rests. I sat with my feet planted firmly on the carpet as if I might get up and go any minute now.

I explained how unfair it was that Marcel's brother died from suicide, seeing how Marcel can't commit suicide even if he wanted to. If he tried to wheel into traffic and stay there, someone would yank him back. There would be no real way for Marcel to carry out a hunger strike because he has a feeding tube and people would just dump food into it whether he wanted it or not. He does not have the kind of body autonomy suicide requires.

But, also, he really wants to live, despite how hard his life can be. He likes being alive. He finds joy in small things—the sun, a chocolate cupcake, watching hockey. He feels things deeply and thinks about complicated problems and wants his life to be better, and those things supersede a wish for an early death. This, I told Dr. G, is what frustrated me the most—my inability to value the life I have. Have I learned nothing from Marcel? What kind of ungrateful person am I? Dr. G asked me if I thought I was being too hard on myself. I told him no.

"You don't blame Marcel for his physical disability." Dr. G said. It wasn't a question.

My instinct was to say *I'm not disabled*. But I stopped myself because that was Dr. G's point—that maybe what's going on in my brain is a kind of disability, and, if I can grant Marcel the space to be himself, if I can offer him my time and patience, can't I give that to myself, too?

I really like Dr. G. His office is the plainest office I've ever seen: beige carpet, white Venetian blinds, a desk against one wall and two wooden chairs with faded pink cushions on the other wall. On his desk is a mess of papers, a cuckoo clock (which I told him was a little on-the-nose) and still, the copy of *Being Mortal.*

"But that's different. He can't help that he has CP."

Dr. G did the eyebrow thing. He said, "You have a lot of patience for everyone except yourself, it seems."

I started to cry, which I'd given up resisting. "I want to be perfect."

Dr. G waited a moment before he said, "But you accept that Marcel isn't perfect."

We went on this way over many more appointments until, near the end of one session, Dr. G asked why I don't write about Marcel, both as a way to memorialize all the things we've been through and as a way to begin to understand the way I see myself versus the way I see him. He's not the first person to suggest this.

"No way," I said. "Writing about Marcel is some kind of appropriation."

He raised an eyebrow.

"It's not my story to tell," I said.

He doesn't bother pointing out that Marcel's story is my story, too, a story of becoming myself through friendship. He knew I'd figure it out eventually. "Have you asked Marcel if he'd like you to write about him?"

I wished I were a better liar. "No," I said.

"Maybe that's a good place to start," he said.

And, because I liked Dr. G and wanted to be a good patient, I knew this was a conversation Marcel and I would have. I was more than 100 percent sure Marcel would say he didn't want me to write about him. Once, Marcel told me he hated when people said he was an inspiration. As if that was all his life amounted to—a totem people could look to and say, *well, we don't have it as bad as that guy.*

Almost a year after my first visit with Dr. G, I was in the car on the way to work and there was road construction. It was nothing major—just some resurfacing or pothole filling. But it made for a lot more traffic, a lot more stopping, slowing, and navigating through orange cones and around people holding slow/stop signs. I was suddenly very afraid that I'd misunderstand the signs, that I'd go the wrong way, that I would hit the flagger or another car or drive my car off the road or into one of the giant, unfilled holes. I was afraid I'd be hurt, that I'd hurt someone else, that I'd be late for work, that I'd damage the car in a way that would cost us a lot of money or a little money and some aggravation or that I wouldn't be smart enough to know how to get my car fixed. Once these thoughts started, it was like emptying a bucket of Legos on a tile floor. My stomach and heart clattered and flashed. I took a breath. And then I started to sing: "*When you're down, and troubled, and you need some lovin' care...*"

Months into therapy, after I'd talked and cried for many hours, Dr. G suggested I find something "fun for the sake of fun." I told him I don't like to do things that aren't productive and that I also might not be good at. He gave me his trademark raised therapist eyebrow.

Because I wanted Dr. G to think I was doing a good job at getting better, I signed up and paid for six weeks of singing lessons. I am a notoriously enthusiastic and awful singer and so singing lessons were something I was sure I couldn't feel too much pressure to be good at. I paid in advance because I'm frugal and I'll keep going rather than waste money. It was a good thing, because I'm terrible at singing and, even though my singing teacher, Matt, was sweet and patient, the whole thing was excruciatingly embarrassing and, if not for the pre-payment, I would have quit immediately.

Usually, Matt sat at the piano. I sat on a stool until he told me to stand because it's better for the breath. I had no idea what to do with my hands while I was standing, so I shoved them into my pockets or folded them demurely in front of my stomach. Sometimes Matt made me look in the mirror so I could see how little I opened my mouth when I sang. I hate looking in the mirror and it's way worse with my mouth open. Always, Matt wanted me to think about moving my breath over my vocal cords and out past my lips. He sang a scale—a kind of *a-ah-ahh-ah-a* and I was supposed to match him. When I got it right, he grinned. Sometimes he clapped.

I told Steve and Marcel about the singing lessons, no one else. Steve, because he would notice I wasn't home on Friday nights and Marcel because I trust him and because I don't like to keep things from him and because I know he can appreciate not being perfect at something and doing it anyway. Still, it's a long time before I tell him about my depression.

The only song I learned at all in six weeks of my singing lessons is Carole King's "You've Got a Friend." Matt was a young and talented teacher who wore bright, floral shirts. When he explained how air moves over the voice box, he gestured to his throat and then drew me a diagram on the little whiteboard that was probably meant to display encouraging phrases or praise for his more promising students.

I told Matt about my panic attacks and my therapy because I didn't want him to think I think singing lessons will lead to land the role of Eliza Doolittle or something. I told him how I was in choir when

I was eight or nine and the choir instructor told me God would prefer if I lip-synched. Matt nodded at all of this, unfazed.

I never got past the first two lines of the song because I have a lot of trouble with pitch. Still, Dr. G recommended I sing when I feel a panic attack coming on, so I do.

The panic attacks got so bad that I started to have them when other people told me about long drives they had to take.

"This makes no sense," I told Dr. G. I was furious at my inability to just get better. It took years for me to make the connection between my patience with Marcel's cerebral palsy and my impatience with my depression, my ability to offer Marcel grace and my inability to believe I deserved the same. I held myself to a standard of unattainable perfection even as I told Marcel he was too hard on himself when he couldn't spell a word the right way or was slow to move his chair. I told him trying was what mattered. It's only through the constant, wry looks he gave me, the knowing way he smiled and nodded his head in my direction when I told him to be nicer to himself, that I began to understand that I could also be nicer to myself.

Dr. G explained about synapses and brain chemistry, and my primary care doctor explained the same thing and I understood it in the way I believe in math—it exists and is useful to some people but incomprehensible to me. I said all the right things to other people who have depression—things like, "Your brain is the same as any other body part," and "You wouldn't feel ashamed if you had a sore knee"—but I still hated that it was happening to me. I felt like a failure.

"But," Dr. G said, "You don't think Marcel is a failure."

This again. "Cerebral palsy isn't his fault."

He raised an eyebrow.

"It's not," I said.

"Depression isn't your fault."

I rolled my eyes.

I finally told Marcel about the panic attacks because I could make them sound funny, especially the part where I sing through them: "*You just call out my name, and you know wherever I am, I'll come runnin', to see you again.*"

Marcel laughed a little and then typed into his communication device that he likes that song. I said I do, too. I felt a little proud that he knew what song I was singing, because sometimes songs sound right in my head but wrong out loud.

Marcel and I sat in the driveway of his group home, him in his wheelchair, me on a semi-broken stool I dragged out from the garage. (The group home lost their case to send him to a nursing home, so he's back home after his long hospital stay, although home is now a place he knows he isn't wanted.) We're supposed to go for a walk, but I have a torn meniscus and it's too painful to put weight on my knee. After he rolled and I hobbled to the end of the driveway, I confessed I was in pain. His face turned to all worry and he immediately about-faced his chair to head back inside. But it was a beautiful day and so I suggested we sit in the garage with the door open so we could get some air but still have enough shade so he could type on his communication device.

After we talked about how our weeks went, I told him my therapist thought I should write about him, about us, about our friendship, and Marcel lit up with pleasure. He lifted his head and smiled and nodded in that way he does when he wants to make sure his assent is known. Yes, he wanted me to write about him. Yes, he trusted me with his story. Yes, he thought it was important that the world know what it's like to live with a disability.

"Really?" I asked.

He furrowed his brow at me, having picked up on my hesitation.

"Well," I said, "It's just—" and suddenly I wasn't sure. I said I didn't want to make assumptions about him, which is what people have done to him all his life. But he shook his head at this. "Because you're sure I know you?" I asked. He nodded. I made him promise to listen to me read everything I wrote about him and approve it and he agreed.

"Okay," I said. "I'll try."

In a perfect world, Marcel would write his own story. But Marcel can't use his hands to write or his voice to speak. He uses a computer—a communication device—operated with a laser on his glasses to type onto a screen and then have a computer-generated voice speak his sentences. Even though it would be difficult and painstaking, he might be able to eke out his story on his communication device. But Marcel never went to school and so he can't read or write much beyond a second-grade level. His intelligence far exceeds second-grade, but he lacks the tools to be able to convey that to the wider world.

I would never write this if not for his urging. Marcel wants his story told so that people can see what it's like for a person with a severe disability to navigate the world. He wants to show you his life and his determination to keep living it. And I want to show you the beauty of his friendship.

Once, when Marcel was in the hospital for a colonoscopy, his gastroenterologist recognized me. He'd been her patient years before in a different hospital and now here we all were again. While I was waiting for Marcel to emerge from anesthesia, the doctor turned to me and told me her daughter has special needs and that, watching Marcel and me together all those years ago gave her hope that someone would see her daughter as the full person she is. I smiled and said I was so glad to hear that, but then I added, "It works the other way, too. He sees me for who I really am. And he likes me anyway." This, I think, is the great gift of friendship.

In the early days of this project, a literary agent told me no one would ever publish this book. Why would they, she said, when there are disabled people writing their own stories? When I told Marcel this, he cried. He cannot tell his own story. The literary agent had a point: There *should* be more stories by disabled people. But the spectrum of disability is wide and everyone's needs are different. Marcel's story deserves to be told, even if he can't tell it himself.

I am telling this story, but Marcel wants it in the world. He wants to be part of the conversation about who gets to take up space, who gets to be seen, who gets to be heard.

How To

A tree is known by its fruit; a man by his deeds. A good deed is never lost; he who sows courtesy reaps friendship, and he who plants kindness gathers love.

—Saint Basil

When Becki called and asked me to bring Marcel to visit her in hospice in 2013, I'd known him for sixteen years but I hardly knew her at all.

"I'm going to tell him I'm dying," she said.

I'd known she was sick, but I hadn't known she was dying, and so for a few seconds, I stammered my condolences, apologies, and assurances that there was still hope, although I had no business suggesting such a thing. And then I fell into silence while I tried to figure out how to get out of bringing Marcel to see her.

Before she got too sick to work, Becki had been Marcel's Speech Language Pathologist. There are very few SLPs in Maine who work with adaptive equipment like his communication device, and only very specific circumstances under which that work is paid for through Medicare or MaineCare, which are the only payment streams Marcel has. Most of the time Becki helped Marcel without getting paid just because she didn't want him to go without the help he needed. She understood him, challenged him, listened to him, teased him, and helped him advocate for himself. Marcel counted on her and loved her.

By the time Becki got sick, Marcel relied on me as well as Becki. We had an established routine of seeing each other every weekend—maybe to go bowling or out to eat, or maybe just for a walk or to watch a movie in his room. I was his Durable Medical Power of Attorney by then and accompanied him to many doctor's appointments. But Marcel could also count on Becki and so, by extension, could I.

On the phone, I hesitated long enough that Becki finally said, "He's going to need you." Did she know that, at that point in my life, I felt untethered? Did she know that, in the years to come, Marcel needing me would be one of the only things to keep me grounded? I like to think she sensed my need for Marcel even while she was looking out for him. That maybe she knew we'd be good for each other.

In the early years of our friendship, Marcel didn't depend on me for anything other than making reservations for a handicapped-accessible bowling lane and driving the van without incident (and even with that I was only semi-competent). I was in my early twenties and not ready to be needed in any substantial way.

I was married when I met Marcel, and my first husband was decidedly uncomfortable around him. The few times they met, he'd stiffen and become formal, polite, unlaughing. I don't know if it was the proximity to disability that made him uncomfortable, of not knowing what to do with otherness, but he flatly refused to join us at the beach or movies or walks. When we divorced in 2001, Marcel was among the first people I told. He told me he was sad for me. He asked if I was okay. I told him I felt like I'd made a bit of a mess of my life and he shook his head adamantly. I was only twenty-six. What kind of woman is a divorcee at twenty-six? What kind of person so royally screws up the plan? A plan made by and known by only me but still one I took very seriously.

Marcel steadfastly continued to be my friend. We went for walks. We went to Kentucky Fried Chicken. We watched *All My Children.* And showing up for him consistently reminded me that I had something to offer the world. Or at least offer to one person in the world.

But now, this afternoon of Becki's phone call, I was nearly forty years old. It was time to step up. I was going to have to, whether I was ready or not.

Seeing no way out of it, I agreed to a date and time to bring Marcel for a visit. A few days later, with as much nonchalance as I could muster, I told him Becki invited him to visit her. I didn't say why. In fact, I told him she sounded great when I talked to her.

The first time I met Becki was an afternoon when Marcel asked me to sit in on one of their sessions. Becki was big all around with a soft face and short, practical hair. She was middle-aged, confident, competent, and I was still perplexed by life—twenty-four, in an unhappy marriage, and selling Mary Kay products, even though I was no good at makeup, because I'd quit my job at the nursing home and needed to make money while I figured out what was next.

That day, Becki and I sat in the nursing home hub on the plastic-covered floral couch and Marcel sat opposite us. She asked him a question and he tried to answer with his voice and she told him to use his computer. "That's what it's there for," she said.

Marcel made a "yeah, yeah, yeah," sound and rolled his eyes and then he turned on his communication device and typed painstakingly while Becki just sat and waited. I had always jumped in to try to figure out what Marcel was trying to say, but this time, I took Becki's lead.

Marcel focused the laser attached to his glasses on the computer screen in front of him. It was a tedious task, controlling his head enough to get the laser to land on each icon on the screen in front of him long enough to select it. Becki seemed to be in no hurry. I, who had been raised to be almost maniacally productive, found the slowness unsettling. I looked around the small but busy hallway where we sat, observed out loud the ringing call bells, the smell of some distant cabbage-y lunch. I got up to check on the old woman who beckoned me over. I came back to the couch and folded and refolded my hands. Becki just waited. She must have found me annoying.

Marcel's communication device has thousands of words and phrases stored in a series of pages that are indicated by icons. He has the sequences of words and phrases he uses the most frequently memorized. The device also has numbers and letters that allow him to spell out words not saved as icons, or words he can't remember how to access. He spells words phonetically, which, because words are often not spelled how they sound, sometimes leads to confusion. Like, he might say he wants *stek* which will sound like *stack* when the device reads it but what he means is *steak*. If he told Becki he wanted *stek*, she would ask him context questions like "is this a place you want to go?" or "is this something you want to eat?" And then when she'd landed on the right context, Marcel would nod and she'd ask a follow-up question, and then maybe another, until she landed on *steak* and then she'd help him spell the word correctly and save it in his communication device for the next time he wants a steak.

I, on the other hand, had been approaching our conversations like a game of darts—I'd toss out words until I landed on one but often not before Marcel gave up in frustration. If he said *stek*, I'd fire back "Stack? Stock? Sneakers?" And then I might repeat "Stek, stek, stek" as if the mere act of repetition might help me figure it out. More often than not, Marcel would apologize and tell me never mind.

Becki had an actual method, one that demonstrated how well she knew him.

I could think of no reasonable way to get out of bringing Marcel to see Becki, and so, on the appointed day, I loaded him into the van and drove to the nursing home where she was in hospice. The whole way down the turnpike, I rattled on about how nice it was going to be to see Becki, how great a friend she was, wasn't it amazing and great how long they'd known each other. I was practically manic in my made-up happiness. Marcel, who hardly had any family involved in his life, who dealt with almost constant staff changes at the nursing home, who had just attended the wake of one of his beloved nurses who died in her early forties from breast cancer—Marcel should not have to suffer more. And now here I was, driving him toward what would certainly be pain and sadness. I'm sure he noticed my strange behavior, but Marcel, in the way back of the van, simply made noises of agreement.

When we got to the room, I greeted Becki with a wave and then said, breezily, "I'll just give you two some privacy."

Marcel gave me a quizzical look.

Becki shook her head. The wig was gone. Her hair was a soft peach fuzz. It had started growing back because they'd stopped treatment, which I knew because she'd told me and now she was about to tell Marcel.

"Stay," Becki said. She pointed to a chair.

Marcel and Becki were about the same age—in their early sixties—and I hadn't ever known a person so young preparing to die. I didn't want to stay and witness Marcel's grief, which would surely translate to my grief. But she said to stay and so I stayed.

The second time I met Becki was when she called and asked me to bring Marcel to her house. She'd been diagnosed with cancer by then and was sick enough that she couldn't come to work at the germ-ridden nursing home. Marcel's communication device wasn't working again and it would be easier for her to fix it in person rather than walk me through it over the phone.

"There's a ramp," Becki said.

What she didn't say was that she'd had the ramp built for herself, not in anticipation of Marcel's visit. By then she couldn't climb stairs because the cancer was in her spine—had always been in her spine, as it turned out—and the pain was immobilizing. She anticipated needing a wheelchair in the coming weeks.

Her house was a plain gray two-story with a new, unstained wooden ramp like a tongue sticking out from the front door. Taking up a solid half of the living room was an antique carousel with the most beautiful painted horses I've ever seen—white and pale pink with gold accents. It was a real, once-working carousel. I can't remember how she said she came to have it but it was the single grand thing in an otherwise cluttered, tired house that smelled of used kitty litter and sour milk. Years later, when I mention the carousel to Marcel, he doesn't remember it. I wonder if I've made it up as some kind of antidote to how sick she was and how terrible I felt for Becki and for Marcel.

Her couch faced the kitchen where dishes were stacked all over the counter. "Can I help with anything?" I asked.

She requested a glass of water and her pills. She wore a wig then, and it wasn't a good one.

There was cat food and cat litter all over the floor of the kitchen. I didn't see how she could bend to clean it, but I didn't know if she'd be offended if I cleaned it. I didn't ask and I didn't clean it.

We sat in the living room and she told us that for years she'd complained of back pain but had been dismissed when she complained because she was obese. It didn't matter to her doctors that she'd always been obese and had never had pain like that. It turned out the pain was from tumors all along her spine. Marcel let out a wail and my throat ached. Maybe he felt the same—dismissed because his body doesn't look like a "normal" body, every ache, every complaint attributed to cerebral palsy with no deeper inquiry. There was no point in being angry, Becki said. It was too late for should-have. At that point, there was hope, and she told Marcel to focus on that.

And now, just a few months later, here we were, settled into her hospice room—Marcel next to Becki's bed, me in a plastic chair as close to the door as I could manage. Becki looked right at Marcel and said, "You know I have cancer and that they've been treating me."

She waited for him to nod.

She went on, calm and even, "They're done treating me now. It hasn't worked. I'm going to die." She never broke eye contact with him.

He started to cry. I swallowed and swallowed and swallowed but finally gave in and started to cry as quietly as possible. By then, I knew Marcel had no family who came to visit and few friends like Becki, who really saw him as the complete, complicated person he is. I knew losing her could only be devastating. And even though I didn't know her well, I relied on her example and her presence as Marcel's friend.

Becki waited for a break in the crying. "I'm not in any pain," she said. We both cried harder. Becki didn't.

She waited for us to calm down. Then she went on to say how much Marcel's friendship meant to her. And Marcel, with his voice, said "Me, too."

"I know," she said, and took his hand. I was desperate to leave the room, to get away from how awful this was for both of them. But she'd told me to stay, so I stayed.

She had a small gift for Marcel—it was some kind of figurine and I can't remember the significance of it, just that it meant something to both of them. She told the story that went along with the object and they both laughed.

Eventually, I relaxed into the stories she told. They both laughed and Marcel cried a little more and she held his hand. I don't know if I realized then, in that moment, that I was being shown how to be his friend, his person.

The day we had visited Becki at her house, she removed Marcel's communication device from its mount and walked me through how to troubleshoot what might be wrong with the device.

I nodded along until I realized she actually expected me to remember what she was doing. "I'm not tech savvy," I murmured. Those communication devices aren't cheap and Marcel relies on his pretty heavily and for sure it couldn't be me who had to know anything when I never even learned how to program a VCR. Becki couldn't be serious that she was going to teach me how to do all this. Besides, she wasn't going to die.

"You're going to have to learn," she said. I protested, but Becki shook her head. She went on to say that she didn't know how sick she was going to get from the treatment. And she didn't know if she'd get better. In retrospect, I think she must have known the treatment came too late and that it wasn't going to work. She said it like we were discussing a possible storm coming through. She waited for me to answer. I said I'd try.

The nursing home had taken a position that they would not touch Marcel's communication device because it was a liability. There were, at the time, very few speech language pathologists in the State of Maine who worked on communication devices. And Becki knew she wasn't going back to work anytime soon and that the likelihood of the other therapist getting Marcel on the schedule was slim. So few of his family members were even marginally involved in his life, he couldn't count on any of them to help when he needed it. It was going to have to be me.

I felt sweaty and sick to my stomach as Becki walked me though the different parts of Marcel's communication device. I had never liked doing things I wasn't immediately good at. I liked success and praise and the instant gratification of an A+. I quit everything I didn't do well in. In high school, it was basketball, track, cheerleading, drama, student council, and choir. I'd changed colleges when I didn't fit in, changed majors when I wasn't the best at the first one, and quit my job when it seemed no one liked me. And now, here was Becki, telling me that giving up wasn't an option. Marcel, watching all this, nodded his approval and encouragement, which I was certain I didn't deserve.

In the van on the way home from hospice, Marcel and I were quiet. He, I imagined, was thinking about the good times he and Becki had shared and the gap that would be left by her absence. I did not ask him. I was feeling determined to not let either of them down. About six months later, Becki's sister called Marcel to say Becki died. She said it was peaceful and that she hadn't been in any pain. Marcel and I cried together.

In the more than a decade since Becki died, our friendship has deepened, in part, at least, thanks to her. I've quit other things—jobs, friendships, that first bad marriage—but I've persevered in many more things—hard things—that I never would have thought myself capable of. I'm still the person who fixes Marcel's computer, and I'm also the person who attends his care meetings, helps him advocate for medical care, and sorts out paperwork of all kinds. I'm better and braver and more competent than I ever thought I could be. And still, every time I have to fix his computer, we invoke Becki. "Come on, Becki," I say, "Don't let me screw this up." Marcel always gives a little laugh-cry and looks up, finding her in his memory.

Speculation

But those sent—or committed—to what became known as Pineland—included orphans, children taken from their poverty-stricken parents, persons with physical disabilities like cerebral palsy, unruly youth, youth or adults convicted of crimes, persons, persons with various intellectual disabilities, the "morally feeble minded," persons who might later have been termed autistic, and sometimes persons with various types of mental illness. Some were non-verbal, some non-mobile. Parents of children with various types of disabilities often were advised to commit their child to the facility, and sometimes to forget about them, which some parents did. With few community-based services until the 1960s, most parents had limited options.

—"Out of the Shadows: The Legacy of Pineland"

I often think about what Marcel's mother must have experienced when he was born. It was 1950, in Lewiston, Maine, and this was her second baby. Though we don't know if her first son, George, was born without complications, he did not, at any rate, have cerebral palsy.

She'd likely had an uneventful pregnancy up until the time she delivered Marcel, and then something went wrong—an umbilical cord around the baby's neck, maybe. Somehow, a lack of oxygen to the brain for what might have only been seconds. Or something may have happened in utero. Even now, there's no prenatal test for cerebral palsy.

In 1950, fathers weren't in the delivery room and so Marcel's mother, Emilienne, would not have been able to feel his reassuring touch, if he was the kind of man to give a reassuring touch. From the little Marcel has told me about him, he wasn't, but maybe that hardness happened later, an accretion of disappointment.

Either during the birth or immediately after, Emilienne would have known something wasn't right. There would have been commotion, much more than she'd have experienced with George, and the nurses would have whisked the baby away, perhaps without even telling her what was wrong. If there was no commotion, if they immediately placed her baby to her breast, I think she would have known something was different just by looking at his face.

I wonder if, at first, they kept Marcel from her. Maybe they said she'd be better off not seeing him, not holding him. In those days, it was common for disabled babies to be institutionalized right from birth.

I like to imagine Emilienne as a kind of warrior, insisting her baby come home with her. Marcel's father must have agreed to it. Because Marcel was not institutionalized, was never institutionalized, and was raised at home.

The term "cerebral palsy" was coined in the late 1800s, and it's likely the diagnosis was given to Marcel within the first year of his life. According to the Cerebral Palsy Foundation, Dr. William John Little first identified and named the condition (originally called Little's disease) in the 1800s. He believed it was caused by a lack of oxygen to the brain. Later in the 1800s, Freud speculated that cerebral palsy was the result of fetal abnormalities. Today, doctors believe both men are probably right—cerebral palsy develops either in utero, during, or shortly after birth. It was not until 1932 that Dr. Winthrop Phelps floated the idea that not all children born with CP have cognitive impairments. Until then, a physical disability equaled a mental disability.

I wonder if Marcel's parents were told he'd die soon. Many parents of disabled children were told that. I think about how hard it would be to let yourself love a baby you thought wouldn't be around long. Conversely, I think of how hard it would be to stop yourself from loving your baby, no matter what.

In 1950, there were some therapies and treatments for cerebral palsy, but they were for rich and well-connected people. Doctors knew little about cerebral palsy and the general public knew even less.

In every case of a child born with cerebral palsy between 1940 and 1970 that I've read about, the parents were encouraged to put the child in an institution. Most often, they were told to forget their child ever existed. Many parents who had means and money sought second, third, twenty-fifth opinions. Marcel's mother had neither means nor money, but she chose to keep him at home.

Did the doctors tell Emilienne to put Marcel in an institution? To consider—to be forced to consider—that her child should be hidden away from the rest of the world? She would have been told it would be better for both of them, as well as for her other, "normal" child. I like to imagine her triumphantly taking Marcel home, like King Arthur with the sword.

But she must also have been terrified. She would have wondered if she was doing the right thing. Wondered if she'd have enough help caring for Marcel. Wondered if she would be taking too much time and energy away from George, who was four when Marcel was born.

At some point, Marcel's parents decided to keep him in bed. It probably seemed safer that way. And it's not like there was a push, at that time, for crippled babies to have physical, occupational, or speech therapy. I try to imagine this, but I get tripped up by the person Marcel is now—a person who hates to nap because he might miss something interesting going on, a person only in bed to sleep between 11 p.m. and 6 a.m. or if he's sick. Maybe all the time he spends out of bed now is to make up for the decade he didn't get to leave it.

Marcel's father, a devout Catholic, believed he or Emilienne had done something wrong to displease God in order get a child like him. I know this because Marcel has told me this, through tears. Some things never stop hurting.

When she took Marcel home from the hospital, Emilienne would have anticipated the help of her large family (she was one of ten siblings). But shortly after Marcel's birth, his father moved the family from Maine to Texas, where he had better job prospects—but no family. Emilienne, George, and Marcel would return to Maine when Marcel was ten, after his father died. That's also the year Marcel got his first wheelchair.

Emilienne likely knew nothing about cerebral palsy until after Marcel was born. She may not have even heard of it. In 1952, two years after Marcel was born, Marie Killilea, whose daughter was born with cerebral palsy, published her book *Karen*. The book, which details everything Killilea did to get Karen seen by specialists, set up with therapies, and as independent as possible, was well-received and helped create an atmosphere of advocacy for people with disabilities. But the family profiled in the book had the resources to take their daughter to twenty-four doctors all across the United States before they found one willing to work with them. They had the resources to create an at-home physical therapy program (an entire gym, really), which was needed because there were no trained therapists anywhere near them in Albany, New York. They had the resources to teach their daughter at home when she couldn't attend school and to get her to and from school when she could. If I had been a French-Canadian woman who spoke English as a second language living far away from family and who didn't have the contacts or money to put in place good medical care and adequate education, the book might have left me feeling that, without money, my kid was destined to have a life of struggle.

Marcel's parents were undoubtedly told he wouldn't live long, which may have been a factor in the decision to keep him in bed. Why make the necessary adaptations to a stroller, a high chair, a swing? All of that would feel like gestures of hope.

Did his mother tell George to be a good big brother? Did she tell him to look after Marcel? Did George resent Marcel, this tiny baby who needed a lot of care and attention? Or did he treat him like a doll? I want to believe it was hard for him to know he could go out and play and Marcel couldn't. Did he turn the radio on for him? Did he carry small gifts in his pockets and show him frogs and rocks and fireflies? Did it bother him that Marcel had to stay in bed and he didn't?

Marcel has George's baby portrait. It's a sweet baby face against a pale blue background mottled with white, probably a department store studio backdrop meant to look like the sky. There was no such portrait taken of Marcel.

In the ten years Marcel stayed in bed, I imagine his mother read to him, washed him, fed him, talked to him. She must have seen how quick-witted he was, how he laughed at jokes, cried at injustices. She must have played the radio and maybe she brought a TV (if the family owned one) into his room or maneuvered his bed so he could see the one in the living room.

I wonder if, in the years Marcel stayed in bed, his mother ever had George help her move his bed outside so he could feel the Texas sun on his body. It would have been hard to do with a bed without wheels, so probably not, but my mind persists with the image. Marcel loves the heat, and his skin turns the color of a toasted almond in the summer. Maybe they carried him outside while his father, Leonard, was at work, settled him in one of those plastic loungers, and watched as he tipped his face up to the sun.

Only after his father died, when Marcel was ten, did Emilienne get him a wheelchair. Once, Marcel told me she thought his inability to propel his chair was because he was lazy, that he didn't try hard enough. Maybe she'd heard by then about other people with CP who had been taught to feed themselves, even to walk with crutches. Maybe she didn't understand that therapies need to start when children are very young. Marcel lost ten years of life spent in bed. That waiting meant his muscles stiffened and atrophied. Or maybe she knew this, deep down, but she didn't want it to be true.

Marcel never went to school. His mother must have known he was smart enough—she would have recognized the understanding in his eyes, the quick laugh he has when someone makes a joke, the way he nods his understanding or furrows his brow to ask for clarification—but I'm sure she worried how he'd get in and out of the building, to and from class. How he'd eat lunch. How he'd go to the bathroom. She couldn't ask George to be Marcel's caregiver, because she must have asked a lot of him already: stay and watch your brother while I go to the store, help me get your brother into his wheelchair, don't let those boys hurt him. There wasn't money to pay someone to be an aide and, even if she had insurance, insurance back in those days wouldn't have covered an aide. Also, she might have had a hard time convincing the school that a physical disability did not equal a mental disability. And even if she could have convinced them Marcel was smart enough, how could she have kept him safe for that many hours away from her? Some kids with disabilities certainly attended school, but there were no laws requiring access until 1973. Kids who went to school would have had to rely on teachers and their fellow students to get up and down flights of stairs, on or off the toilet, or to eat lunch. Marcel could not only not walk or use his hands, he also couldn't talk. School would have been nearly impossible.

Emilienne would have grown up hearing the words "retarded" and "feeble-minded." She might have been aware of the law in Maine, enacted in 1925, in the era of eugenics, that required the developmentally disabled to be sterilized. She would have likely known about the Pownal State School, which was not far from where she and George and Marcel lived in Lewiston after Marcel's father died and they returned to Maine. It was an institution of over seven thousand patients, many of whom were a lot like Marcel.

The first time we visited Marcel's parents' graves, when I was twenty-five, I learned that George died at the age of thirty-nine. "How did he die?" I asked. We're gazing down at the flat metal markers of his mother, father, and George. (His stepfather, Gerald, is buried in a Veterans' cemetery.)

Marcel tried to say it with his voice: "He-hess-shon."

I had to say it several times, slow and then fast, before I got it: Depression. George died of depression. "You mean," I asked warily because I didn't really want to know, "that he killed himself?" I had never known anyone who died by anything other than old age. I didn't know how to talk about suicide, other than with the anger and then avoidance my mother met me with when I made a rather weak attempt to kill myself at sixteen. Anger didn't feel right in the face of Marcel's grief, and so I was at a loss for not just what to say but what to feel. It was only in later years that I would have coworkers and friends who lost parents, children, and spouses to suicide. It was only later I could begin to see George not as selfish but as suffering.

"Yes," Marcel said, and then began to cry.

I'm guessing Emilienne knew George was depressed, and possibly, based on what Marcel has told me, had bipolar disorder, although she wouldn't have had the word for it then. She knew he could be angry and volatile—Marcel has told me he was, at times, afraid of his brother. I don't know if she ever thought he might take his own life. That his sadness and anger could be so uncomfortable, could make him so desperate, that he believed death was the only option. She must have spent so much time trying to keep Marcel safe and alive that it may not even have occurred to her that her able-bodied son would die first.

Emilienne's plan might have been to have George take care of Marcel if anything ever happened to her—that was the way of families, especially close-knit French-Canadian Catholic families like theirs. She'd remarried after Marcel's father died but didn't have more children. George died in January of 1986. Gerald, Emilienne's second husband, died that June. The grief of that year must have been almost too much to bear.

But she did bear it. And so did Marcel.

In the 1950s, '60s, and '70s, there would have been no great expectation for Marcel's life span. Surely, his mother didn't think he'd outlive his father, brother, and stepfather. She must have thought she, at least, would outlive him. But she didn't.

Emilienne died of lung cancer in 1990. She was seventy-five. Maybe she and Marcel talked about what would happen to him when she died. He was living on his own by then in an apartment in Portland, but still she must have worried what his life would be like without her keeping an eye on him. Most of her siblings were still alive and her brother, Gil, must have assured her he would take care of Marcel. Which he did, faithfully, until his death in 2008.

I don't know what I would have done if more than one doctor told me to put my kid in an institution, to give up, to expect his early death. I don't know what I would have done if doctors and friends and neighbors and fellow church-goers gave me pity but little else. Marcel's mother somehow not only continued to mother her son until she died, but she also found joy in what had to have been a hard life. I've seen photographs of the two of them laughing over a birthday cake, in his stepfather's truck, in big, awkwardly posed family pictures. I know she didn't have all the answers, maybe not even all the questions, but she loved her son, and she never stopped trying to make a life for him.

I think I would have liked her.

We Are Family

Walking with a friend in the dark is better than walking alone in the light.

—Helen Keller

When we met in 1997, your Uncle Gil was your emergency contact. He's the person who bought you sneakers and peanut butter cups. At least twice a week, he came to visit you in the nursing home where I was the Activity Director.

The first time we met, I was struck by how young you were. I was used to people in wheelchairs, people who had aphasia, people who needed to be fed. Mostly, though, I was used to those people all being old. At the time of your admission, only one other guy anywhere near you in age—you were forty-seven—lived in the nursing home. He had AIDS, but I don't think he was in the nursing home because of AIDS but rather because of some mental health issues. He and I talked, briefly, but he mostly stayed in his room.

You came to bingo, to music programs. You were bright and quick—making a noise if I missed covering a bingo number, listening to music with your whole body leaned forward. Maybe a year after we met, you asked me to help you learn to read and so we began spending an hour once a week in the conference room. It was a small, damp-hot room, and the reading material left by your tutor was childish—Frog and Toad books, mostly. You and I decided to abandon those books, and you asked for the biography of Loretta Lynn. I told you I hate country music and you hesitated, worried you'd asked me to do something I didn't want to do. I saw how kind you were, how thoughtful. I told you I could suffer through, and you laughed and I knew we had a similar sense of humor. It took us months to get through that book, me holding the book in one hand, pointing to the words with the other hand. In the end, I gained a lot of respect for Loretta Lynn, who it turned out was a tenacious survivor, and when I told you that, you looked pleased with yourself.

We took breaks from reading so I could rest my arm and my throat. You typed into your communication device and the automated voice spoke. We talked about growing up with strict, Catholic mothers. We talked about what we liked to eat. We talked about where we grew up—you in Texas and Lewiston, Maine; me in Massachusetts. I asked you which town in Texas but you didn't know how to spell it and after I went through a few guesses—Dallas? Austin? Fort Worth?—you made your noise of frustration and I said it didn't matter.

After almost two years in a role I really wasn't suited for, I decided to leave my job, and when I told you, you cried. I promised I'd keep coming to visit, but you didn't believe me. You'd been told that before—by family, by caregivers, by friends. You believe it's too difficult to be around you because you have cerebral palsy. I, because I was young and very optimistic and naïve, told you everyone has something wrong with them and that some of it is just more obvious. At the time, I thought you thought I was sensitive and smart, but the truth is you probably thought I was simplistic. When I look back now, I find my statement borderline offensive. The list of things you have to rely on other people to do for you is long and in no way compares to the fact I need contact lenses and can't eat blackberries. It's hard for people to be your friend because they don't know what you'll need or how much you'll need. I didn't understand any of that.

After I left my job at the nursing home, I continued to show up every week and we read together. You thought I was doing it for you, and I was, to some degree. But I was also doing it for me, because I needed to be anchored, needed to be expected at a specific time and place, needed to be appreciated by someone. When you got sick of reading, we went for walks. Eventually, you asked if we could go bowling so I borrowed the wheelchair-accessible van and drove you to the alley, and you told me you needed the ramp and I learned how to do handicapped bowling. We went to see Christmas lights. We went to the movies and out for Chinese food and to the mall.

In 2007, Gil got sick. You asked me to take you to see him in the hospital. I loaded you in the van and it was only as we're going that I realized I didn't know where St. Mary's Hospital was. This was years before we all had GPS on our phones. You, in the back of the van, made a noise. "Left?" I asked. "Yes," you said. It was in that moment I realized you knew your way around Lewiston even though you'd never driven. That you'd been paying attention your whole life. That you could find a way to give me directions if I listened.

I listened. You got us to the hospital. I parked and you shook your head and then typed into your communication device that I was in the wrong parking lot. I figured the hospital couldn't be all that big. I told you it was fine, largely because I hated and still hate parking and I didn't want to try to move the big van when I'd just settled it into a spot. When we got to the entrance nearest where I parked, the receptionist informed me we needed to go out and all the way around the building. We ended up having to walk a city block to get to the correct entrance. I admitted you were right and you rolled your eyes at me. I should have trusted you to know what you were talking about, but even then, ten years into our friendship, I sometimes made the mistake of underestimating you.

Gil was very sick. He was in bed, and he was so touched you'd come to see him, so grateful I'd brought you. Your Aunt Leta was there, too. I left you to visit with them went to get a coffee.

When I got back, Gil told me he was grateful for my friendship to you. He said your family hasn't been as involved as they should be because no one wanted the responsibility of taking care of you.

I said that's too bad.

"We've done our part," Leta said. I thought Leta was saying that because she didn't want Gil to feel bad about dying. I didn't realize she was bowing out.

A few days after our visit, Gil died. You asked me to take you to his wake. When I arrived to pick you up, you were wearing dress pants, a button-down shirt, and a tie unlike your usual sweat pants or brightly patterned shorts and t-shirts. I told you you looked handsome. You puffed yourself up like a peacock, and I was touched by your vanity.

At the funeral parlor, there were two wakes happening simultaneously. I peered into each one. I didn't see Leta, and she was the only person in your family, other than Gil, I'd met. At that point, we'd known each other for more than a decade. Yet I recognized not a single person, because your family were all strangers to me.

I signed the guest book. It turned out to be the wrong guest book. It was for the other guy, the other family I'd never met.

You shook your head and rolled into the room where the correct wake was happening.

Your uncles and cousins and second cousins said how good it was of you to be there, how wonderful you'd come, how good you looked. They hadn't seen you in years. They'll stop in, they said. They'll have to stop in. They live nearby, they said, but you know how it is with kids and work and everything, just everything.

After Gil died, someone needed to be Marcel's emergency contact and within a few weeks of his funeral, Leta and Marcel had a conversation in which she suggested me. One day in his room, Marcel asked me if I'd take on the responsibility. I was flattered. I had no idea there would be actual emergencies and I would actually be contacted.

A few years later, when Leta's forty-five-year-old daughter died from a drug overdose, Marcel asked me to bring him to the wake. Steve was available that evening, so we both brought him. Leta was touched Marcel came. She told him he was such a great guy. She got tears in her eyes. Marcel had seen her a handful of times in the years since Gil died, all of them because he asked us to take him to see her. By way of excuse, she said she was old and that it was hard for her to get around. She said this without any irony, even though they were about the same age and Marcel is in a wheelchair he operates with a joystick. In retrospect, I see that Leta must have been grieving and likely had nothing left to give to anyone, even a nephew she was very fond of. In three years, she lost her husband to cancer, one daughter to a car accident and another to a drug overdose. It was easy to forget Leta's grief because she always seemed booming with good cheer. I know better now.

At the wake, two of Marcel's male cousins came up to us and they were so happy to see him. They clapped him on the back. They said, "Remember when we were kids and we took you sledding?" "We used to do some crazy stuff," one of them said. "Your mom used to get so mad at us," the other said. "She used to tell us to be careful with you," one said. They were smiling and Marcel was smiling and laughing. Steve and I stood off to the side. This is so nice, we thought. This was the first we'd really heard about his childhood.

And then one of the cousins said, "I should really stop by and see you sometime. I drive by the nursing home every day and I just never think to stop."

Marcel stopped laughing. He nodded. Next to me, Steve went very still. Later, when we were alone in the car, Steve said, "Why say that? Why say, basically, that I drive by you every day and never stop?" I agreed that it felt mean, even though I don't think Marcel's cousin meant to be mean. It was just that it was the same thing that was said at Gil's wake—by this cousin or another, I don't really know—and nothing came of it. Nothing would likely come of it this time, either.

A few months later, I asked if the cousin had stopped by. Marcel said no. I asked again a year later, and the answer was still no. He never ended up stopping by. Marcel was in that nursing home for nineteen years.

I'm not sure when Leta told me you have something like sixty cousins within a fifteen-mile radius of where you lived. "None of them want to get too involved," she said by way of explanation. The idea, I guess, is that if they came by to talk to you or go for a walk or take you out to dinner or church or to a family reunion, they'd end up as your emergency contact. No, that's my knee-jerk, unkind reaction. It's more likely that they feel awkward around you now that you aren't children together, now that you don't have the immediacy of family and play. What is there to talk about when your lives are so different? How can they tell you about their wives and children and jobs when you're stuck in a place that smells always, faintly, of urine.

On the other hand, it seems impossible for your family to believe I genuinely like you and enjoy spending time with you. That your disability is problematic only in the sense that it's problematic for you.

That, yes, I'm the keeper of your medical information, but it's not more than I'd do for my parents or stepchildren or husband. And you make me laugh. You make me slow down—literally and metaphorically. You tell me when I'm wrong to fight with my parents. You're very aware of what's going on in the world, politically and otherwise, and we share a lot of the same perspectives. Many of my opinions have been honed after talking to you. You give me advice about work. You roll your eyes when I cry really hard through almost every movie we watch, even animated ones. You still give me directions when we go places. You buy me chocolates for Christmas and, once, a sweatshirt that says "Happy" on it. You always get the door for me when there's an automatic door opener. You remember things I tell you and you ask how Steve's shoulder is, how my parents are, how my knee is. You always send us birthday cards. You get a ride and show up at my MFA graduation, surprising me. Once, when I get a salad and it comes in a taco bowl, you insist I send it back because you know I can't eat gluten. When I say I can eat the inside without touching the shell, you yell at me with your voice. In this way, you insist I treat myself with the same care I usually reserve for you.

We like to eat out, we like to go for walks, we like live music. We love people-watching. We like hockey. We like musicals. We love Christmas. We like ice cream and dogs and sunbathing. We love coffee with cream and sugar. We stop and smell every lilac we come across in early June.

It's too hard to distill a friendship down into why it works. Besides, I don't have to justify any of my other friendships, so why do I have to justify this one?

I am not your friend because no one in your family wants to be involved. I am your friend because you were the first person I'd ever met who was entirely, genuinely himself, with no pretenses and no airs. I liked your sense of humor, your quick wit, your unfailing kindness.

Perhaps that's because of the cerebral palsy, or maybe it's just who you are as a person, or maybe the two things can't and shouldn't be separated. You were the first person I'd ever met who was entirely himself and the first person I ever tried being entirely myself with. I could try to drive the van through a drive-through, get it stuck, back us out, and, blushing wildly, go in and confess at the nursing home why there was now a scratch on the borrowed van. A less-better version of myself, a version without you, would have left the scratched van in its parking spot at the nursing home and pretended I knew nothing about it.

In the earlier years of our friendship, I could tell you about a fight I'd had with my parents and then, hearing it out loud, admit I'd been not my best self. I could, when you asked for my help programming your VCR, confess I didn't know how but I'd read the manual and give it a go. I could admit how ridiculously proud of myself I felt when I actually programmed the stupid thing. I even did a little dance and, when you laughed at me, I laughed, too.

Sometime after the funerals but before we'd entirely given up hope of family visiting Marcel, we were eating out at a restaurant Marcel picked. We were at our table, and I was feeding him and we were talking when he looked over at the table next to us and got really excited. "What?" I asked. I thought maybe he spotted a celebrity and I was wondering if my hair was okay.

A woman stood from that table and came over to us. She said, "Hello, Marcel. I haven't seen you in ages. You look well."

He asked how she was with his voice and when she stood there, perplexed, I said, "He wants to know how you are."

"I'm well," she said. "Getting old," she said."

Finally, she looked at me, then Steve. "Are you his help?" She asked.

"His friends," I said.

She gave me a look I interpreted as both skepticism and resentment. She didn't introduce herself. She went back to her table, and when she left, I asked who she was. "Cousins," Marcel said. The whole table was full of his cousins.

Marcel's cousin Amy started working at the nursing home just before his sixtieth birthday. I'd been planning a surprise party for him for months. I hired a country singer named Vicki Lee, rented the VFW hall down the street from the nursing home, planned the menu, and started inviting people. I'd even purchased hockey-themed invitations.

Amy found out what I was planning. It wasn't a secret—it wasn't meant to be a secret—I'd already asked Leta for a guest list, which was probably how Amy found out. Amy cornered me one afternoon and told me family should be the ones planning the party, and I couldn't argue with that. She told me to back off. She was angry about it, and I didn't get why—I still don't. Still, I cancelled the singer and the VFW hall. Marcel's family came to the party Amy threw, which was held in the nursing home's activity room. I fed him cake while his family talked to each other, mostly.

Marcel watched them. He was smiling, happy to be in their presence. I wasn't sure what to feel about them. They seemed like nice people. Talking with their hands, laughing, touching each other's arms. But there was always that gap of floor space between Marcel and them, and I disliked them for not trying to pull him into the conversation, for not asking how he spends his days or how he's feeling. They were there, at least, and he was so happy.

During the time Amy worked at the nursing home, Marcel asked me to help him clean his room. We went through drawers and I held up t-shirts or sweaters or sweatshirts and asked if he wanted to keep it, donate it, or throw it away. Amy found out about this and confronted me in the hall one day. She told me *family* should be going through Marcel's things. Even though I felt like I was being accused of something—but what?—I told her that was fine. I didn't bother pointing out she was the only family I'd seen anywhere near his room in ten years.

She cleaned his room, throwing out, among other things, the hockey-themed quilt I made him. Marcel apologized. I wondered if she even asked him if he wanted it thrown out. I wondered if she held it up and asked if it should be kept or tossed. I told him not to worry about it.

I don't know—then or now—if Amy was being deliberately hurtful to me or Marcel. I have the feeling she was just reacting to the family's lack of involvement by being strangely defensive. Guilt can make a person do odd things.

Soon after that, Amy left her job at the nursing home and Marcel heard from her once or twice. She said she was very busy. She said she'll stop in soon. After a Christmas card some years later, he never heard from her again.

One of Marcel's cousins owned the laundromat that's just down the street from the nursing home where he lived. It was less than a mile away, but on the opposite side of the street from the nursing home, which meant we had to cross four lanes of traffic. There was a crosswalk but no light.

When we got to the laundromat, we were told his cousin was on vacation. We left a note. When she returned, she called and left

Marcel a message saying she was sorry she missed him and she hoped he'd come again.

A few years later, we make the same trek. That time, when we finally make it to the laundromat, we're told his cousin had sold the business.

"Did you know that?" I asked Marcel as we walked back to the nursing home.

He shook his head. It was a dumb question, because if he'd known the cousin sold the business, we wouldn't have walked all that way. Maybe, the cousin didn't call to tell Marcel of the sale because she didn't think Marcel would make the trek again. Or maybe she just didn't think of Marcel at all.

Every time Marcel is in the hospital, the nurses and doctors and social workers ask if we're family. "Just friends," I used to say. Now, I say, "Friends." It doesn't need a qualifier.

In 2015, Marcel had surgery to remove all but an inch of his colon and put in an ileostomy. In the days leading up to his surgery, he asked me to let Leta and his cousin Michelle know what was going on. I messaged them. They replied with thoughts and prayers.

On the day of the surgery, Leta asked me to keep her posted. I suppose she meant well, but I was anxious and in no mood to appease anyone else's fears. I told her Marcel was my first priority. I told her I'd be at the hospital all day. This was when all I had was a flip phone and no way to send Facebook messages when I wasn't home.

Leta said that was great, so good of me. Keep her posted!

I messaged her when I got home after Marcel woke up from the anesthesia. I let her and his cousin Michelle know what room he'd be in. I had only met Michelle once, at Gil's wake. Marcel told me her mother and his mother had been very close.

A few weeks later, I heard from one of Marcel's other cousins. She said she was sorry they hadn't been to see him but their father, Marcel's uncle, had been very ill. He died within the next few days, and Marcel told me to message them his condolences. I did. The cousin sent a thank-you message. She said Marcel's a great guy. I reminded her he was still in the hospital, but there was no more mention of visiting. I'm sure they were dealing with their own grief, catching their breath after their father's illness and death.

When Marcel finally left the hospital, nearly three months after he went in, not one family member had been to see him. I believe his family cares about him, and that they're busy with their own lives. I also know how much it hurts him that they don't make an effort to see him.

After his ileostomy hospital stay, Marcel moved from the nursing home in Auburn to a group home an hour away in Chelsea. A couple of years after the move, Leta messaged me to ask for the address. I messaged her back that his email and Facebook accounts hadn't changed and that she could ask Marcel directly for his address. My refusal to just give her the information was pointed and mean and not my best moment. I was hurt on behalf of Marcel, but here was Leta, wanting to reach out. Who was I to be Marcel's guard dog? When Leta didn't respond to my snarky message, I asked Marcel if he wanted her to have his new address, and he, always nicer and more forgiving than me, said yes. He doesn't expect to hear from anyone, but he also hasn't given up hope.

I sent Leta his new address.

Sometime after that, Marcel's cousin Michelle messaged me to say she got his address from Leta and she planned to come visit. For the next several months, I asked if Marcel had seen her or heard from her. He hadn't.

Four years later, in 2019, Marcel moved again. This time, he's geographically much closer to his family. Still, they didn't come. Then the pandemic happened which ended nearly all visitations everywhere. Even so, Marcel and I never missed a week—we visited outside with masks or we chatted through Zoom.

Does the fact of our friendship allow your family to justify their absence? I think so. I believe my presence makes them comfortable with their absence. I wonder what would happen if I just stopped showing up for your meetings, stopped going to the hospital and doctor's appointments with you, stopped hanging out with you every week. Would they show up? Maybe, but likely not. And I'd miss you. Our friendship is not something I do out of charity.

It would be nice for you if they came to visit you, though. It's been twenty-five years since you and I met, but still, we wonder what's wrong with your family. Steve and I can't stop ourselves from saying it to each other: Why don't they just come? Just sit with him? Just talk for a bit? Send an email, even. Maybe a phone call. He'd love it. He'd love it so much.

Their loss, *my mom always says. Sometimes it doesn't feel that way, though.*

(Re)create

A public entity may not discriminate against an individual, exclude an individual from participation in a service, program or activity of that public entity or otherwise deny to an individual the benefits of a service, program or activity of that public entity by reason of the individual's race or color, sex, sexual orientation or gender identity, age, physical or mental disability, religion, ancestry or national origin.

—Maine Human Rights Act

It was 2013 and we were at the casino, a place Marcel loves. He loves the lights, the noise, the people. He really likes to win, although he almost never does. Only once, years from this day, will he win the two-hundred-dollar jackpot. He'll ball his fists and scream-laugh with sheer surprise, sheer pleasure.

Today, he wanted to get a casino card. This card gets inserted into every machine a person plays and lets you earn free slot play or points to be redeemed for lunch. Steve and I have cards and Marcel has been using them because he isn't here often enough to earn many points and, once he signs up for a card, he'll get all kinds of junk mail.

He wanted the card, though. So, we stood in line while Steve went off to save us a place at the Top Star machine.

This casino is small, and it felt like everyone was in line at the same time. Some people made a little extra room for us. Some people cut in front of us like they couldn't see us. Each time that happened, I turned to Marcel and asked conversationally, "Can you see me?" He laughed, and sometimes the person who just cut in front of us looked embarrassed. They never returned to the spot behind us, though.

When it was our turn, the woman at the counter took Marcel's information from his ID. She entered everything into her computer and then indicated the small computer pad bolted next to the window. The stylus was attached to the little pad. "Sign there, please," she said.

Marcel and I looked at each other. I waited a beat for her to look up. "He can't," I said.

She stared at me. "If he wants a card, he has to."

"I mean, he physically can't," I said.

His arm won't lift that high and he can't hold a pen, anyway. "He has a stamp," I said.

His signature stamp was made decades ago, before I met Marcel, when he had a bit more muscle control in his hand and arm. It is his signed signature made into a stamp and it works in most situations so that he doesn't have to put some kind of childish X on paperwork, which he really can't do without someone basically moving his arm. In this case, he couldn't even do that because the pad is too high.

"He needs to sign the pad," she said.

"Can you print out the paperwork so he can use his stamp?" I asked. My heart was pounding because people were looking at us and we were holding up the line and this woman, with her severe black hair and red lipstick, was getting annoyed. I was trying to be reasonable. I was trying to come up with reasonable solutions.

This whole transaction should have taken five minutes and now was dragging on and people were in line waiting to cash in their chips or ask how many points they have for the buffet.

"He needs to sign the pad," she said again.

"How about if I sign the pad for him?" I asked. This is not ideal, because Marcel has a stamp and I like him to be as autonomous as he can be. But we wanted to get moving. I glanced at him. He didn't shake his head, which I took to mean he was fine with me offering to sign.

"Do you have a card?" she asked.

"I have a card." I saw where this was going. "He doesn't want to use my card," I said. "He wants his own card."

"In order to get a card, he has to sign the pad," she said. She said this slowly, as if we're stupid. She looked at the line behind us. I deliberately did not turn around. I put my hand on Marcel's back in a kind of "we're in this together" gesture.

"Can we see a manager?" I asked.

Asking for the manager usually gets us a solution. This worked a few months earlier when his house manager refused to color Marcel's hair, something he'd been having done for decades. The excuse was that the house manager didn't believe in using any product with chemicals in it. I tried to reason with her, pointing out the chemicals in nearly everything we use—deodorant, shampoo, Bengay—but she wouldn't budge. Coloring his hair was something the house staff at the previous group home had done, so we knew it wasn't a company-wide policy. Finally, I went to her manager and Marcel's hair turned from gray to black overnight, just like it always did, thanks to the miracle of Just For Men.

Now, Marcel's body slumped forward because he was tired and tired of how hard things were. Already we had to do some tricky maneuvering so he could play a slot machine, removing the chair in front of the slot machine he wanted to play as well as the one next to it, then having him back in. I had to move the red velvet stanchions for him to get in this line.

The woman shrugged. "He's just going to tell you what I told you." She pointed at Marcel. "He either signs the pad or he can't get a card."

At this point, I would have liked to tell this woman and the entire casino to go fuck themselves. We come to the casino maybe twice a year, for no more than two hours at a time. Marcel can only push a button with the side of his hand, and he has such poor control that I have to contort my body so that I cover the "max bet" button with my cupped palm. He's hit it by accident before and, seeing he's on a tight budget and not overly lucky, it makes him run out of cash faster than he would otherwise. And because he doesn't like to take money from me and Steve, losing money makes the day end faster.

I looked at Marcel and he made no move to turn around and leave the line, which would be my cue he no longer wants the card. So, I asked again if I can sign it for him. "He's right here. He'll watch me go over and sign it. I have his permission," I said. I sounded a bit desperate because I was very warm and I would like to take my coat off and drape it over the back of Marcel's chair, but I didn't want to draw more attention to us. The woman was shaking her head before I even finished.

Finally, the woman asked, "Are you his Power of Attorney?"

I'm not. I have Durable Medical Power of Attorney, but that's only in the event Marcel can't make his own medical decisions. I became DMPA in 2008 after his Uncle Gil died and he asked his

Aunt Leta who should be his DMPA now and she suggested me. I'd known him for a decade at that point and, other than Gil and Leta, had not yet met anyone else in his family. Power of Attorney, unlike DMPA, implies Marcel needs someone in charge of his day-to-day decision making, which he does not. But no manager has materialized, and the line has gotten longer and there's only one other window open and I'm getting hot. And, really, how will she know? "Yes," I say. I don't look at Marcel when I say this, but he doesn't make a protest noise so I know he's okay with this outright lie.

"Why didn't you say that before?" She seemed both annoyed and relieved.

For one split second, I thought she was going to ask me to prove it. Which I couldn't. Do people carry Power of Attorney papers around with them to casinos? Or anywhere? She didn't ask. I signed the damn pad and he got his card, and the woman was all thank you and have a nice day. She said this to me—not him—which pissed me off even more.

To the woman, Marcel said "Thank you" with his voice, which meant a push of air that vaguely resembled the sounds in "Thank you."

"He said 'Thank you,'" I said. It was reflexive on my part to interpret when Marcel uses his voice-voice and not his computer voice. I knew he really did want to thank her. Because he's nicer than I am. And because he's used to this kind of discrimination. It's not that he accepts it, because it still makes him feel small and sometimes makes him cry, but he also knows that being nice, that saying "Thank you" is better than telling them to fuck off, which Marcel would never do because he doesn't have a single swear word programmed into his communication device. He doesn't even have a phrase like "buzz off," which would be at least a little satisfying, because he's learned that being nice is safer than being angry. Also,

Marcel was raised to be deferential and polite, in part because of his disability, but also because his parents were devout Catholics. Because I don't want to embarrass him or make life harder for him, I almost never say what I really think of people, either. Not in front of them, anyway.

The woman smiled weakly at Marcel's gratitude. Her eyes were on the next person in line.

We left the line and I felt gross. I shrugged off my coat and carried it until Marcel wagged his head to the back of his chair at which point I used his headrest as a hanger. "I'm sorry," I said. He shook his head by which he meant it was fine. We did what we had to do.

By saying I have Power of Attorney, I confirmed everything this woman and a lot of people think about people who have disabilities—that they can't make their own decisions, that they need guidance to even know what they want, that she is not wrong to stick to her narrow understanding of narrower rules.

I did it because of the line and because Marcel wanted to get to play some slot machines and because it must have been ten thousand degrees in that casino and I was sweating. But I shouldn't have. I should have stayed right there in that line until the manager came and maybe they even had to call their lawyer. I should have said no, I'm not his Power of Attorney because he doesn't need a Power of Attorney. What he needs is a reasonable accommodation and you are going to provide one. Period.

What bothers me more than anything about this interaction is the woman's lack of humanity. I get that there are rules she has to follow—probably pretty strict ones because it's a casino and there's a lot of money floating around. But she could have looked at Marcel. She could have acknowledged, even in some small way, that the casino's policy isn't set up for people who look like him. She could have made eye contact with him and said something like, "Let me see what I can do" or "I understand this isn't great." Anything to show she gets that he's a human being and not just a problem.

We met Steve at the Top Star slot machine and he got up and moved the chair and Marcel maneuvered up to the machine. "You guys were in line a long time," Steve said.

"Long story," I said.

I'd tell Steve on the way home, but for now I wanted to not think about the smug look on that woman's face, the way she knew she could wield her power, the way she could hide behind policy as if, behind it, we couldn't see that she was being discriminatory. I wasn't going to rehash it now because Marcel only had two hours before his support staff took him home and he just wanted to have fun.

Marcel and I go out about once a month, sometimes more, and sometimes less if the weather is bad or Marcel is in the hospital. Still, it works out to an outing about once every thirty days. Multiply that by the twenty-three years we've known each other and that's 276 outings, more or less.

We go bowling, to hockey games, to play bingo, to look at Christmas lights. We attend concerts and comedy shows, basketball games, baseball games, movies. We go to car shows. We people-watch at Old Orchard Beach and the Old Port and Fort Williams. We walk and roll on rail trails and downtowns and river walks. We go to the mall and the Dollar Tree and Walmart. Once, we went handicapped skiing, which it turns out Marcel hates. We went to a taping of *The Price Is Right* when it was on the road here in Maine. We eat out a lot.

Often, we get seated without a problem. Often waitstaff and security guards remember Marcel and greet him, if not by name, then by "Hi, buddy." Sometimes it's easy to find handicapped parking. Sometimes people slide a table or even the metal detectors out of his way so he can get through narrow openings. But just as often, people pretend they can't see him and let the door close in his face, or they fail to step aside or they walk right in front of him. Displays are placed in ways that make it impossible for him to go down an aisle. Handicapped seating is often so narrow his chair won't fit and I have to sit slightly behind him because I've had to move back the folding chair, which is the seat I pay for to be next to him. And, yes, we ask for accommodations. We ask and we ask and we ask.

Marcel asked to go to Longhorn, probably because he saw an ad on TV. We'd never been, but it was a big, new restaurant, so I figured we'd be okay. By which I mean there wouldn't be a step, two doors with no automatic door openers, or doorways so narrow Marcel would bloody his knuckles trying to scrape through. I don't call ahead, which I usually do, but it turned out to be okay—it was an easy roll up to the big, wide, automatic door-opener door.

The hostess, who was nineteen, maybe twenty, took one look at Marcel's chair and said she was sorry but she couldn't seat us. I stared at her. "The chair won't fit," she said. She was completely serious, as if her inability to seat us was absolutely our fault and she was being sweet about how we'd inconvenienced her by even asking for a table. I can see now that she hadn't been trained to get help when she encountered an unfamiliar situation.

I made a noise that was like a laugh, but Marcel and Steve knew I wasn't laughing. "No," I said.

The hostess fidgeted the menus in their slots. She looked at the floor, at the door, at the crowded room.

Granted, the restaurant packed tables in so tightly the wait staff had to turn sideways to wedge themselves and their lofted trays from one diner to another. There was, however, within my line of sight, a baby stroller at a table. The hostess didn't send them away. Also, the restaurant setup was not our fault.

Quietly, even though my heart was hammer hammer hammering with both anger and nerves, I said, "You may want to go get your manager before you say anything else and I have to call the ADA."

By "ADA" I meant the Americans with Disabilities Act, which I was pretty sure was not a thing I could call. I'm not a bluffer by nature, so that moment was one of my proudest.

We waited as the hostess scuttered off to consult with a manager, which she should have done in the first place. Steve wanted to leave. He said we shouldn't give Longhorn our business after this. I agreed, even though I kind of wanted to stay to make a point. But Marcel wanted that steak he saw on TV. The hostess returned from her consultation with the manager and—imagine that—there was a table for us. The table was tiny and so close to the kitchen that if the wait staff didn't watch it, they'd swing out the door and trip over Marcel.

"I'll sue them if they spill something on you," I said. I didn't mean it, but I was pretty riled up.

Marcel shook his head, calm as always. He knew I was just blowing off steam, but he also wanted to make sure I didn't actually sue anybody.

Marcel ordered the filet, rare, with mushrooms, double mashed potatoes, extra gravy, and coffee with five creams and five sugars. I sliced off pieces of steak as big as I dared (never as big as he wanted) and fed him. He asked for more salt, more pepper, more salt. He devoured nearly every bite. When he finished eating, I gave him coffee through a flexible straw.

The waitress never came by to see if we needed anything and only perfunctorily asked if we wanted dessert. Even though she was walking away as she asked, Marcel did want dessert. He ordered a chocolate-peanut butter cake/ice cream dish and finished nearly all of that, too.

Steve and I vowed to never go back to Longhorn, and we don't, until a year or so later when Marcel asked to go again. *Really?* We asked. *Yes,* he said. That steak was really good and he wanted it again. And so, we went and when we got to the hostess station, I thought I might pass out from all the nerves coursing around in my blood. But, it was a different hostess and, while she hesitated at the sight of his chair, she did not refuse us a table. She seated us in the middle of the room, dropped the menus, and fled.

It's not like this every time we go out, just most of the time. Maybe not most. Some of the time.

It was 2014 and Marcel wanted to go bowling and he wanted his friend Jack to come with us. I called the bowling alley, and the person I spoke to told me they don't reserve lanes unless it's for a birthday party.

"It's two handicapped men," I said. "It's just for an hour."

"Then they can't reserve a lane." The guy on the line said. He was borderline rude, but I was trying to be better about ignoring small slights.

"Is there any way you can make an exception?" I asked. "It takes a lot of planning to get them there and it would be so disappointing if they can't bowl."

He assured me that if we come on Sunday at ten in the morning, it'll be fine. If I had children, or if I ever went bowling, I might have realized this was likely untrue.

We borrowed the van, which, since the nursing home changed its policy, we now paid $25 a day to use and can only use on weekends if no one else is using it. We loaded Marcel and Jack into the van, which required having each of them wheel onto a lift (one at a time), raising the lift, having them roll forward, hooking four hooks on each of their four wheels and then fastening a seatbelt over their chest and the chair. We got to the bowling alley, unstrapped and unloaded them both, and rolled in right at ten.

No, the woman behind the counter told us, we can't have a lane. "There's a birthday party today." Of course there was.

"We'll just be an hour," I said. "There's no one here now."

"They're coming," she said. "There's nothing I can do."

"Please," I said. "It's a whole project for us to get here. Please. One lane, just an hour."

She said the party would be over by noon if we wanted to wait. That would get us home after 1:30 and the guys couldn't wait that long. There would be lunch to eat, bathroom needs, pills to take.

We left.

Later, I wrote a letter to the owner of the bowling alley. I told him I understand policy, and I understand his employees were following policy. The guy on the phone who told us it wouldn't be a problem, the lady who wouldn't let us take up a lane reserved for an invisible birthday party. It probably doesn't say anywhere in the policy that on Thursday when someone calls asking about renting a lane and you tell them it's all set for Sunday, you might want to check to see if there are any birthday parties booked for said Sunday. I suggested in my letter that it might be a good idea to train employees to sometimes, occasionally, when the situation requires nuance, use their discretion.

About a week later, the owner called me. He apologized and asked what he could do to make it better. I was shocked by his call and suspicious of his sincerity. I figured he thought I could be smoothed over with nice words. He said he'd send me a coupon for three free strings. He said I could call anytime and reserve a lane. He said he changed his policy and spoke to his employees. He said this was his fault, not theirs.

We waited a month or two before we called to book a lane. I had Steve do it, in case they flagged my name. But when we got there, they knew who we were anyway and they apologized for the inconvenience of our last visit. They let us reserve a lane. Now, whenever we call, we can reserve a lane.

We made a difference. That's something, isn't it? Not really, because it turns out that other bowling alleys have the same no-reservation policy and we run into this again and again when Marcel moves and starts over in one new city and then another.

We drove to the South Portland High School to see Josh Blue, a comedian who has cerebral palsy. He won some competition—*America's Got Talent*, maybe—that Marcel watched. Marcel heard from someone that he was touring and we looked it up and I bought us tickets. The handicapped ones, as always, were the most expensive aside from front row.

We got to the high school early, parked, then walked and rolled around the campus until the doors opened. The woman who took our tickets at the door gave us a long, mournful look. "The elevator is broken," she said.

She waited, as if we were expected to apologize for the need of the elevator. Finally, I said, "Is there a backup plan?" I didn't bother asking when the elevator broke, because it was probably not just a minute ago.

She looked over her shoulder as if the plan might be just about to arrive. "I'll see what I can do," she said. Perhaps she thought we would just leave. Perhaps she didn't know we had to pay for the van and drive an hour and a half to get there. Perhaps she thought Marcel could walk if he tried hard enough.

We were asked to wait and we did. The auditorium filled. If I were to guess, I'd guess they wanted us to ask for a refund and go home. Marcel looked at me and Steve and said, "I'm sorry."

"Did you break the elevator?" I asked, nudging him teasingly.

He shook his head and rolled his eyes.

"Then there's nothing to be sorry for," I said.

The woman was gone a very long time. People streamed into the auditorium, streamed by us as if we were part of the architecture. No one asked if we needed anything.

When the woman returned, she said she can seat Marcel at the end of an aisle, but it won't be the aisle Steve and I sit in because that will be upstairs.

"Can't you ask the people in the aisle where you seat him to change seats with us?"

She looked aghast. "We can't do that."

"Why not?"

"They paid for these seats."

I waited a beat. "So did we," I said.

"Yes," she said. "I know. But there's nothing I can do about the elevator."

I was furious, but I wanted us all to have a good time. How were we supposed to be laughing in half an hour if I was this angry right now?

We helped Marcel park at the end of the aisle so he was as close to the seat next to him and as not-in-the-way as possible. I lingered until the people who had the seats next to him showed up. "Would it be possible to switch seats with us?" I asked. "The elevator is broken and our seats, the handicapped seats, are upstairs. He can sit here, but they told us we have to sit up there." I might have sounded desperate.

They were an elderly couple, although they seemed to be able to get around okay, and they immediately agreed. They were happy to switch seats. They seemed kind and gracious. The woman who initially seated us suddenly reappeared and glared at me.

"Thank you," Marcel said with his voice and before I could interpret what he said, the elderly woman smiled. "You're welcome," she said. "Enjoy the show."

Is it socially inappropriate to inconvenience able-bodied people but totally fine to dismiss handicapped people? I don't know why I'm asking. Evidence suggests yes.

I called the bingo hall where Marcel wanted to go. "Are you handicapped accessible?" I asked the old man who answered the phone.

"Oh, yes," he said. "There's just one small step."

"We can't do steps," I said.

"It's small," he said. "Just a couple of inches. You can bump a wheelchair over it."

I thanked him and hung up. There's no point in trying to explain that Marcel's chair is several hundred pounds and that, while I might be able to get him down the two-inch step, I would not be able to get him up it.

An oversight is just a mistake, right? Not an unkindness. Not an act of discrimination disguised as ignorance. Is discrimination only the willful act of exclusion? Or is it systemic? Ignorance isn't discrimination. Is it?

One argument I hear in response to my frustration is that we can't accommodate everyone all the time. This is a premise I don't totally accept, but I will concede that some spaces were created before ADA laws went into effect so, yes, maybe those spaces can't be changed to accommodate everyone. But we could just listen more to other peoples' needs. We could just pay attention. We could try to see each other.

The doors at Applebee's were glass and there was no automatic door opener. It would have been okay if there weren't two sets of doors—one that opened into a short vestibule and one that opened into the lobby. Two sets of doors are tricky because we can't let one go to get the other without running the risk of it slamming into the handlebars of Marcel's chair and cracking.

There are laws about handicapped accessibility, but is this part of that?

We were early—it was just after the restaurant opened because it's easier for us to get situated if it's not crowded.

I was behind Marcel, giving his chair a push as he throttled forward to get over the slight lip at the door. Steve was holding the first door with his foot while stretching his 6 foot 2 frame to get the other door open. At the hostess stand, a hostess and waiter both watched us impassively.

Marcel wheeled far enough inside that I could use my butt to hold open the first door and Steve could scoot himself forward to get the second door. Marcel rolled slowly through. He didn't want to run over our feet.

When we got all the way in and the doors swished shut behind us, Steve said to the hostess and waiter who hadn't moved, "Did we look like we were all set?"

They blinked at us.

"We could have used a hand," Steve said. "Getting in."

"I'm sorry, sir," one of them said. "You could have asked."

I suppose that's a fair point. But should we have to ask to be seen?

We were at Walmart because it was Christmas and Marcel wanted to buy a present for every person who cared for him at the nursing home. He had a list of twelve names and only thirty dollars to spend. He wanted to find those little tins of butter cookies, which he guessed would cost about $2 each. Past the Salvation Army Santa, into the bright lights and Christmas music, we aimed for the aisle we thought the cookies might be in.

A woman with a cart brimming with stuff—gifts, presumably—materialized right where Marcel turned. He tried to turn the other way so she could get by, but she corrected the same way. He realized his mistake, but now he was nervous, and when he gets nervous, his muscles tense up. And when his muscles tense up, he has less control. At that point, he could barely move. Instead of laughing at this cart impasse, the woman grew furious. She pointed at Marcel and barked, "I need to go that way."

Usually, we keep our cool. But this time Steve lost it. It was Christmas, for God's sake. Steve said, "Why don't you try sitting in a wheelchair all day for just one day and see how it feels? Don't you think he'd love to be you for even just one day, walking around, shopping for presents?"

I was proud of Steve for coming to Marcel's defense, but I was also nervous. I didn't want Marcel to be upset. I didn't want to make a scene. I didn't know how mad this woman was or what she was capable of.

The woman barely even paused to register what Steve said to her. She didn't look at Marcel. Instead, she swerved around us without another word. We all looked at each other.

"It needed to be said," I said.

Marcel nodded. I put my hand on his back and we went to get the cookies.

Am I exaggerating when I say that it seems like people would prefer you stay home where they don't have to see you? Where they don't have to be reminded that a lack of oxygen to the brain for less than a minute at birth can cause a person to have a disability which makes it so he can't walk, talk, or even scratch his nose with any accuracy. They'd also rather not know that your brain works fine. It's easier for them to believe you don't know what's going on. That you don't care.

We went to a restaurant called Antigoni's, which, until Marcel told us about it, we'd never heard of. Marcel liked the subs, Steve loved the pizza, I usually got one of their big, elaborate salads.

This time, Steve held the door and Marcel rolled in and there was a family set up dead center of the room. The dad saw us and stood. "We'll move," he said.

"We're fine," I said. "We can go around."

We could—there's room.

"No," he said. "It'll be easier for us to move."

He stood and his whole family stood and they took their pizzas and salads and plates and sodas and moved to the table in the corner.

It took a while with pushing back chairs and gathering jackets. "Thank you," we said. We had time to say it several more times before they resettled in a corner.

He was being nice, this man, and this story is one we'll tell again and again in the future, an example of how not everyone is terrible and thoughtless. And it's not like he made a big thing about moving. But there were five or six people in his group with three or four pizzas, plus salads and paper plates and brown and orange sodas sloshing about. The chairs scraped and the family fumbled with purses and jackets and here, here, they said, here you go.

We wiped down the table. We thanked them again when they left the restaurant. We were subdued and maybe chagrined.

Maybe the man could have just quietly asked us if we could get by okay. Maybe he could have said, "Do you need us to move?"

Everyone watched his kindness—the cooks, the cashier, the other customers. Everyone watched us settle into the spot so recently, so kindly vacated.

He leaped up to do something because he recognized how hard it is to navigate Marcel's chair through small, crowded spaces. He saw the tilt of Marcel's body, the crook of his hand. He was just trying to be nice.

What is it I want, exactly? Not to have policies that work against Marcel, or to have no policy at all. Not to have people ignore him, or be angry because he's in the way. I want him to be seen, but I also don't want him to be gawked over. To be made a spectacle of.

Still, kindness is better.

We were at the 99 Restaurant and the waitress said to Marcel, "My son has a communication device. How does yours work?" And then she waited while he turned it on and showed her how things are stored in a sequence of icons.

This waitress, unlike most other waitresses, asked him what he wanted to eat. Most of the time, servers asked me what he wanted and I turned to him and asked, "What do you want, Marcel?"

This waitress waited for him to answer. She brought us a flexible straw without me having to ask. She didn't talk overly loudly or in a sing-song voice. When she came with our plates of food, she asked Marcel directly if he needed anything else. While Marcel moved his head to connect with his icons to type, she waited. She didn't look at me for help, to hurry him along. I can't remember if Marcel asked for more gravy or if he said he didn't need anything. Either way, he thanked her.

She said, "You're welcome." She said it just like he's anyone else.

I won't lie—I teared up.

We tipped her 100 percent.

Familiarity equals kindness. That's a start.

We were at an antique car show and Marcel made a bumpy, jolting bee-line to a car he recognizes from his childhood. I'm bad with cars, but it was some kind of Chevy. A '56? '57? I don't know, but he did, and he headed over, me swaying along behind him.

He got up close to the car but stayed far enough away so that no one looked at him like his metal chair and lack of muscle control could be bad news for their very expensive paint jobs.

"Is this a car you remember from when you were a kid?" I asked.

Marcel's communication device works with a laser pointer and so it doesn't work in the sun. He grunted "yes" with his voice.

"Did your mom have one?"

Yes, again.

The man who owned the Chevy we've stopped in front of heaved himself up from his lawn chair. He was all smiles.

"His mom had one like this," I said to the man.

He looked at Marcel. "You can come closer," he said.

Neither of us moved. We knew it cost these car-restorers years and a lot of money and Marcel doesn't have great control of his chair, especially on uneven grass.

The man opened the driver's side door. "Come right over here," he said.

I said, "He probably shouldn't. He doesn't have great control." Marcel hadn't put his chair in gear yet.

"It's okay," the man said. "Come on, I want to show you."

So, he went. Slowly, and with me holding my breath. The man ushered Marcel so he was nestled between the driver's seat and the door. And then he told Marcel what he'd done and how he'd done it. Just like he'd tell anyone else who loves old cars.

Joe

What's in a name? That which we call a rose by any other name would smell as sweet.

—William Shakespeare, *Romeo and Juliet*

It's 2018 and you're in the hospital again, propped in bed with pillows keeping you from listing to one side or the other, and I'm sitting on a pink pleather chair I've pulled up next to the bed.

We watch "Dr. Phil" until 4:00. I always find this show melodramatic, but you seem riveted. You want to know about these people, their lives, their lies, what they'll do with the information unveiled to them.

When Dr. Phil signs off, I switch on the Classic Country music station, and we talk. I tell you about a colleague who was in line to change her last name back to her maiden name, and the woman in line in front of her was legally changing her name to Dinosaur. We both laugh at what it would be like to go through life being called Dinosaur.

I tell you how when I was a kid, my friend Caroline and I played teenagers, and my pretend name was always Bonnie. Bonnie seemed like the name of someone with long blonde hair who had a lot of fun. Maybe I was thinking of Bonnie and Clyde. Bonnie was decidedly not like Jennifer or even Jen. There were at least three other Jennifers in every one of my classes. Not a single Bonnie.

"Have you ever wanted a different name?" I ask. I expect you to say no. I expect you to say you like your actual name, Marcel, because it has a musical lilt to it and it's unusual, although surely more common in the French-speaking community you grew up in.

"Joe," you type into your communication device.

"Joe!" I say. I'm completely flabbergasted. Just a regular Joe. Joe Schmo. I'm sure I've met a hundred Joes, and I can't recall any of them offhand. Joe is a medium guy with medium-brown hair and an unremarkable chin.

"Why Joe?" I ask. But already I'm comparing my medium-Joe with your jutting chin, your loose mouth, your build which is on the small side of medium and, because you can't stand, makes you seem smaller.

"It's regular," you type.

A prolonged and mysterious bout of vomiting brought you here to the hospital three weeks ago. Now you've finally progressed to food classified as soft solids—macaroni and cheese, mashed potatoes with gravy, chocolate or butterscotch pudding, one milk and one chocolate milk.

When I came in today at 2:00, your lunch was sitting on the rolling table next to your bed. You can't feed yourself. You've never been able to feed yourself. Cerebral palsy is your primary diagnosis, listed first in your chart, and so presumably the nursing staff is aware that you need someone to feed you. Although I should know better than to presume. The tray sat there, untouched, within reach—if you were a person who had the necessary motor skills.

"Did you not want this?" I asked you.

"No," you said with your voice.

"No, you didn't want it?"

"No," you said again. I waited, and you typed into your communication device that no one came in to feed you. You didn't ring your call bell because the nursing staff has told you that you ring it too often.

I rang for the nurse.

"No one came in to feed him," I said.

"We're short-staffed," she said.

"He can't feed himself," I said.

She checked the electrolytes you're getting intravenously as if that made the whole not-feeding-you situation a moot point.

"Fed and nourished are two different things," I might have said, but didn't.

I wasn't about to feed you milk that had been left out for hours. You didn't want it, anyway.

I wonder if Bonnie and Joe would have gotten along. Bonnie, with her long blonde hair, her flowy hippie shirts, her bangle bracelets. Joe, who would still have your black hair, of which you're proud enough to have the gray dyed out, your olive-to-walnut-with-a-tan skin, your dark eyes, your perfect ears. Joe would wear jeans instead of elastic waist shorts or sweatpants, button-up Hawaiian shirts instead of t-shirts, natty mahogany brown loafers instead of white socks and leg braces.

Bonnie would have all the social graces. She'd easily ask questions and follow-up questions of strangers at parties. Joe would be able to feed himself whenever he wanted and whatever he wanted. He would be able to get up and get a snack on his own or order a meal at a restaurant without typing it into a computer using eye gaze technology. He'd like concerts, but also just being home by himself, reading or flipping through TV channels. Joe would go out on dates, get married, have kids. Bonnie would be single, flirtatious, an outrageous gift-giver and world traveler. They might never even meet.

I know what my alternate persona is like, but I'm imagining yours. That day in the hospital, I didn't ask you to describe Joe, because I thought it might pain you to picture a life in which you could walk and talk. But that's not true because I know you must think of that all the time. I just don't hold space for it because I don't know what to do with feelings I can't somehow fix.

Here's the thing about the way you grant me friendship: I can try again. When the next chance comes up to listen better, to leave space for you, I can do better. And the opportunity does present itself one day when we're watching "Crip Camp," a documentary about a camp for disabled kids in the 1970s. Two of the participants have CP, meet at camp, fall in love, and have a son. You start to cry. You tell me you always wanted kids. I say, "It must have been really hard for you to not get to have kids." And then I shut up and listen.

Here, in your hospital room, though, I say, "Marcel is such a good name. You don't like that you stand out?"

I regret it as soon as I say it.

I want to be Bonnie so that I'm not weird and bumbling, so that instead, I'm unique and confident bordering on reckless. You've always stood out because cerebral palsy makes your legs flaccid, your hands curled, your arms only semi-controllable, your face loose around the jaw and your breath inadequate to activate your vocal cords. There's nothing you want more than to blend in. To be a regular Joe.

"No," you say, a bit teary now. You use your voice to say it, not looking at your communication device but at me. In my make-believe, Bonnie is hard-hearted, acerbic, self-centered. If you were yourself and not Joe, you would be the one to soften Bonnie, the one to make her laugh at herself.

"My mother named me after the dead girl in 'Love Story,'" I say. This fact has always made me a little angry because it seems like my mother gave up on me before I was even born.

But when you laugh, I laugh. "Who names their kid after a dead girl?"

I'm trying to distract you from want, from longing. I'm trying to not acknowledge your sadness by papering over it with my own.

"Were you named after someone?" I ask. I imagine it was someone your mother adored, someone aspirational. Naming children after a saint is something Catholics do, so maybe you were named for Saint Marcel, who was alleged to have slayed a dragon. I will refrain from imagining your CP as the dragon.

You shrug.

"A relative?" I ask.

You nod.

"That's nice!" I say, with so much enthusiasm my teeth ache.

I imagine Dr. Phil asking me what's really going on here. Onstage, with the lights on me, the cameras, Dr. Phil's excessive empathy, I would say that I don't want you to want to be someone else, because it means your otherness bothers you. I want you to be okay with being yourself, even if I'm not okay with being myself, and even if I understand why you'd be frustrated with the life your body limits you to.

"I like that you're unusual," I say. "It's nice to not be like everyone else."

You shake your head. "No."

Photographic Evidence

> *As a culture, we are at once obsessed with and intensely conflicted about the disabled body. We fear, deify, disavow, avoid, abstract, revert, conceal, and reconstruct disability—perhaps because it is one of the most universal, fundamental of human experiences. After all, we will all become disabled if we live long enough.*
>
> —Rosemarie Garland Thomson, *Seeing the Disabled: Visual Rhetorics of Disability in Popular Photography*

I buy Marcel a replacement digital picture frame—his first one broke, though none of his group home staff knows how. In the absence of involved family, I've become the keeper of his pictures—a few albums, a box of loose photos from his aunt, a handful of framed pictures he has no room for.

Scanning the pictures is tedious, but a pleasant way to get to know different parts of Marcel's life. Later, when the pictures are loaded onto his digital frame, he and I will sit in his room and watch them scroll by together.

In one photo, Marcel sits in the yard with his dog, a white fluffy thing as tall as his lap. His arm is stretched toward the dog and both he and the dog are smiling. I asked the dog's name, but Marcel didn't know how to spell it and so I made a few feeble guesses: Fluff? Puff? Rover?

"Can you tell me what letter it starts with?" I ask.

Marcel thinks for a minute and then shakes his head. So many letters sound like one another: B, C, D, E, G—It's hard for him to know the right way to begin and a wrong guess could keep us at this for more minutes than he cares to spare.

There's no one I can ask about the dog.

It bothers me that I don't know, in part because I really want to know, but in part because I think of how frustrating it must be for Marcel to hold so many of his stories inside. To not be able to say something like, "Do you remember the time [name] chased that skunk up the tree?" To have to rely on people who have the shared memory to tell the story. And when they're gone—through death or by choice—the stories go untold.

Here, Marcel is young, mustached, and standing. He's wearing jeans and a white button-down shirt next to a pretty blonde woman with hair I would have died for in 1985—a big wave of sprayed bangs, a cascade of crunchy curls.

"You could stand!" I ask. I don't try to hide my surprise, my incredulity. I see what I'm doing here—fetishizing his ablebodiness. I have, with my delight, reinforced the idea that standing is better than sitting. That if you can't stand, you are not as good, or at least not as delightful.

Marcel makes a noise like "eh."

When I look closer at the picture, I see the blonde woman has her arm behind Marcel, holding him up, and that he's leaning back into her. She was his therapist, he says. "Physical Therapist?" I ask. He nods. Standing, even at a lean, requires more muscle tone than he has in his legs now, more than he's had in the twenty-five years I've known him. Standing must have felt like a huge accomplishment, something Marcel worked hard for. He could stand, even for one brief moment. How proud he looks in that picture.

I did a semester at a school that specializes in documentary studies. They taught us that if we were ever invited into our documentees' homes, we should ask about their pictures. Pictures get people talking. But what if talking is hard? What if stringing the words together to make sense of a memory means landing on icon after icon after icon, sometimes forgetting which icon leads to which sequence of words and having to back out and start again and again and again. And doing that makes your neck muscles ache, your head feel foggy, your whole body sag from exhaustion?

Two pictures are of Marcel's mom and stepdad, Gerald, in a passionate embrace. Both are slightly off-center, as if the picture-taker didn't want to be seen or didn't want to interrupt the moment. In both, Emilienne and Gerald are intertwined, him leaning into her, her tucked in his arms.

"They really loved each other, huh?" I say to Marcel one afternoon as we watch the frame scroll through. He makes his yes noise.

Marcel has two iterations of his parents' black-and-white wedding picture framed on his wall—one of them standing, one seated. Both of them are wearing suits, hers lighter-colored than his, her wearing a hat at an angle, both of them facing slightly to the side of the camera, neither of them smiling. Emilienne in her wedding picture—posed, beautiful, still. I imagine they also loved each other, but, at least in the picture, it seems like a more reserved kind of love than the kind she shared with her second husband.

In Gerald's embrace—nearly hidden by his face on hers, Emilienne is just a pouf of white hair above the slick black of his, her whole body dipped back, her hands around his head, the floral wallpaper of the kitchen or the light from the living room window off-center behind them.

She had two sons when she married Gerald, and one of them was severely disabled. It must have been a hard life, and yet these pictures feel joyful.

I imagine the person taking the picture smiling, blushing, maybe telling them to knock it off but not really meaning it. I wonder if it was Marcel's brother George who took the pictures. Marcel has never said how George, who would have been fourteen when their father died, felt about Gerald, if they got along. Marcel adored his stepfather, and I like to imagine they were all a happy family, but he's told me his brother was unwell and unpredictable. That he sometimes had violent outbursts. That Marcel was often scared.

I like to believe George had good moments, too, and that taking these pictures, seeing his mother so happy, might have been among them. I like to imagine Marcel beside him as he raised the camera, a co-conspirator.

Here, Marcel is the passenger in a white truck, the rounded front giving away that it's an old truck, an old picture. He looks twenty, maybe.

I love this picture because Marcel seems so normal and so happy. But the opposite of normal is abnormal and I want to fight against that, even in my own head, the idea that a disability is abnormal. And yet, that's my reaction when I see the picture—joy at his joy, joy at his regular-ness.

He doesn't get to sit in the passenger seat of vehicles anymore. He's not as light as he used to be, but the bigger problem is that he's institutionalized now. He's gone from a nursing home to a group home, which is less tightly regulated than the nursing home, but there're still a lot of rules in terms of how his body gets moved from one place to another.

These days, Marcel rolls into a handicapped-accessible vehicle, get strapped down by hooks on each wheel and one big seatbelt across his body and the chair. In this photograph, he's turned toward the open window, head thrown back, laughing. His mother is in the driver's seat, peering around him at the person taking the picture. She isn't smiling, but her expression is one of satisfaction. The sky around the truck is crystal blue.

Next, Marcel and his stepdad are in the kitchen. They're both facing the camera and I imagine Marcel's mother taking the picture, of her coming in from doing some laundry, maybe, and finding the two of them talking in the kitchen, telling them to turn this way so she could capture the moment. This was before Marcel had his communication device, when all he had was the flimsy push of air over vocal cords that only produces words for people who really know him. Gerald has his hand on Marcel's back, between his shoulder blades and he's leaning slightly forward, conspiratorially. His mouth is a little bit open, like he's midway through telling Marcel something. Based on Marcel's wide, laughing face, it's a joke or funny story. They are both wearing white short-sleeved polo shirts. They both have black hair. Gerald has a soft mustache, Marcel has glasses. Easily, they could be father and son.

Marcel asked me, once, for pasta with egg scrambled into it and I, astonished, asked how he knew about that dish. It's a meal my Italian grandmother made: orzo cooked and drained and then, while the pasta is still hot, an egg scrambled into it. Generous amounts of butter, parmesan cheese, salt and pepper stirred in. My Nana made it for my father, and then me. Marcel said his stepfather used to make it for him.

In the picture, there's a plant hanging from the ceiling, lush and full. And there's a curtain across the doorway where a door might be, a striped curtain—peach, brown, and yellow—on a tension rod. At first, I think the curtain is decoration, like the plant, but then I realized Marcel's mother must have hung it there so he could get from one room to another without having to ask someone to open a closed door. I imagine curtains strung across the doorway to his bedroom, too, or maybe that was a room shared with George, who might have preferred a door.

Emilienne probably didn't know anyone else who had a child with cerebral palsy, and yet she figured out a lot of things. I find this comforting, even though, or maybe because, I know she wasn't perfect. Marcel says she was too overprotective, but I understand her overprotectiveness. Marcel isn't fragile, but the world is not an easy place for a disabled person and back then, in the 1950s, '60s, even '70s, it was much less accommodating than it is now.

Marcel is in the kitchen again, this time leaning forward from the waist, a kind of curl upward and out of his chair that looks like joy and not effort. I'd guess he's in his early twenties. He's leaning toward a slice of birthday cake—chocolate with chocolate frosting, his all-time favorite—that has been decorated with a row of lit candles. His mouth is open in a kind of laugh-blow. Marcel doesn't now and didn't then have the muscle control to purse his lips or blow air through them, but the joyful expression on his face says he's going to give it a go.

Maybe this is when I should say he doesn't have any teeth. His parents had them all pulled when he was little. I only asked about it once, back when we were still getting to know each other. He told me they had them pulled because they thought it would be too hard to care for them. Maybe they were advised this was the best course of action—to prevent possible tooth aches and problematic dental visits (Marcel can't keep his mouth open). Marcel's parents had his teeth pulled in one session or two; I asked but I didn't ask him to clarify when I didn't quite understand. I didn't want to think about it, but I did ask if it hurt. Which is a stupid question. I've had a single tooth pulled and it *hurts*—if not during, then after. The pain of one tooth multiplied by sixteen or thirty-two, makes me a little panicky just to think of it.

By the time I met Marcel, it'd been decades since his teeth were pulled and his gums are as hard as teeth. He can chew steak, potato chips, salad, anything, really. I don't know why his parents didn't have dentures made for him. I'd guess they didn't have the money and probably didn't think he'd live long enough to really benefit from them. By the time they realized he wasn't going to die in childhood, his gums would have been too scarred for false teeth.

There's an abundance of photographic evidence of the people who have been important to Marcel in one way or another, people who have come and mostly gone. There are pictures of camp counselors from the thirty-five years he's been attending Pine Tree, a camp for disabled people, pictures of family members I've never met and some I've met only briefly at wakes and funerals, pictures of people who have taken care of him over the years. There are Christmas card photos of babies who are probably adults by now. There are pictures of Marcel in a Halloween costume (a face of scary makeup he said he didn't really like), a picture of him with a person in a rabbit costume, pictures of him at birthday parties a decade apart, balloons tied to his wheelchair both times. There are pictures of Marcel with Priscilla, who was one of his dearest friends in the nursing home. There are pictures of him and his friend Jack at a friend's wedding, both of them in button-down shirts and ties.

The first picture I have of the two of us together was taken in the hallway of the nursing home. We're on our way to the little conference room where I will hold a book and read to Marcel and he will try to learn to read by looking at the words and listening. This is the beginning of our friendship. We'd sit for two hours and read and take breaks to talk about how our days were going—him, frustrated by the quality of food in the nursing home, me, frustrated by my parents. Then we started going for walks around the neighborhood—probably at his request. And then we went to the movies, to hockey games, to the mall, out to eat. Marcel had a lot of ideas about places where he wanted to eat, movies he wanted to see, clothes he wanted to get at the mall. Over time, I started to notice and suggest places and activities: outdoor concerts, bingo, walks along wide, paved trails. I don't remember exactly how it all unfolded, but it was just the same way any friendship comes to be—because we had similar beliefs, a similar sense of humor, similar frustrations and interests. In the picture, I am twenty-three, my hair the dark dark brown I once came by naturally. That day, we'd come down the hall and there was one of the Activity Coordinators, smiling, holding up the camera. Usually I say no, no thank you, I hate having my picture taken. But Marcel stopped his chair so that I almost tumbled into him. He sat up straight, puffed out his chest, tipped up his face, and smiled. The hallway was too narrow for me to scootch around him, and besides, he was so happy. So I stood, my hand on his chair, giving in to his request to be in this picture, in this moment.

With Marcel, I'm more inclined to agree to have my picture taken. Maybe because he likes it so much, I feel ashamed of myself for hating the way I look in pictures. For my endless self-scrutiny. There's a picture of and me and Steve and Marcel when we took Steve's kids to Funtown and Marcel had to pay to get in even though Funtown had no way to get him on any of the rides. When I asked the ticket lady if they could waive his fee, she said she had no way of knowing if he was faking his disability. It was an incredibly insensitive thing to say, but I had no comeback. We paid the thirty dollars and tried to be sincere in our hope that she would never have to face a disability or the accusation that she would be the kind of person who would fake one.

There are a bunch of photos of us at Pine Tree through the years—unpacking the van, sitting in the treehouse, on the boat, on the foliage-dappled paths through the woods. There's one of us with my parents when we all went up to Fast Eddie's because we knew my parents would get a kick out of the old-fashioned car hop. There's one of us in front of the sign an able-bodied person can put a face through from behind to look like a teenager from the 1950s. There's a picture of us when we went with Marcel to the Special Olympics and he won the silver medal for a wheelchair race and I cried and shouted, which embarrassed—but also delighted—him. There's one of Marcel and Steve from one of the times we went bowling. It's one of my favorites because, even though it's of the two of them from behind, it's clear by the way Steve's pointing, by the way Marcel has his head turned to Steve's arm, that the two of them are in serious contemplation about the best way to angle the ramp and place the ball. There's Marcel and me at my graduate school graduation, a surprise he engineered. Marcel and his friend Dave planned it. Marcel was there to see me give one of the graduation speeches and then, later, walk across the stage and receive my degree. Mid-speech, I heard him all the way across the auditorium make the noise he makes when he's emotional—the kind of emotion that is often both happy and sad. I felt it, too, a kind of overwhelmed joy.

The most recent picture I have, to date, is of me, Marcel, and Steve on the pontoon boat at camp. It's July 2024 and the sky is crystal blue with cottony clouds, the water calm. We're all wearing life jackets. Steve and I are bent forward, Marcel between us, reclined a bit in his chair. His hairline has receded a little, and my hair is no longer its natural shade of dark dark brown. We are all a little sleepy from the lobster rolls we ate at lunch, the heat, the sun. It's been a hard few years for Marcel and for us as witnesses to the things he's gone through—hospitalizations so serious we feared he would die, problems with his housing situation, a pandemic that prevented us from visiting him as much as we wanted to. But here, in this picture, in this moment, we're happy.

These Things Happen

Basic disability etiquette involves treating people with disabilities with respect. For example, speak to the person directly, not to the person accompanying them. Do not make assumptions about what they can or cannot do. The impact of a specific disability can vary widely from person to person, so offer assistance only if it appears to be needed. Acknowledge and respect the individual's ability to make decisions and judgments on their own behalf.

—National Disability Navigator Resource Collaborative

Marcel asks to take a walk through the sleepy neighborhood behind the nursing home. It's a decade into our friendship and we're comfortable with each other, easy in our conversation as well as silences. I walk, he rolls. I talk, he listens. The sun is warm, but not so hot that either of us is sweating. Not so hot that I worry he'll get woozy. Like the time he denied he was hot until I insisted we go into the over-chilled nursing home where he threw up and the nurse looked at me like I was irresponsible and I reminded her that he can make his own decisions, even when I think they're bad ones.

I remind her we're just friends, as if there's anything diminutive about friendship. What I mean is I'm not his caregiver, his Power of

Attorney, or his mother. He is his own person. We're just two people who get along. And I treat him like I'd treat any other friend—I ask if he's okay in the heat and he asks me back and I say yes and when he nods in return, I believe him.

We're an unlikely pair on the surface, maybe—Marcel, in his fifties, me in my thirties. Marcel, with cerebral palsy, talking with a communication device, navigating the streets in an electric wheelchair operated slowly with the use of one semi-able hand. Me, never having had so much as a broken bone, talking almost constantly and gesturing wildly while I explain and interpret and consider out loud.

Still, we have a lot in common. Both raised Catholic by mothers who worried a lot. Both lovers of food. Both lovers of sun and heat, music (although he likes Classic Country and I'm an 80s Rock girl), puns, people-watching, dogs, and walks and rolls outside.

On this day, it's bright and I'm not worried about anything. It's a nice day, and there's no one else out. A few distant cars, a few times I've nudged him away from the middle of the road or the soft sucking shoulder at the edge.

I'm talking and so at first I don't see that the young, loping man who has come out of his house is heading toward us. From the corner of my eye, I notice him saunter down the pavers, through the overgrown shrubs, but I think he's going to his car or the mailbox. His house is white, without shutters. There's a dog barking somewhere but not one I'm worried about. We both like dogs, but sometimes they don't know what to make of Marcel's chair and they bark or growl at him. Usually, the dog is with an owner and the owner yanks the dog away, looking astonished and abashed, as if the dog is responding to his disability and not simply the oddity of his chair. As if the dog is expressing its owners' discomfort. "It's the chair," I usually say, to make them feel better. Sometimes, though, the dog is alone, with no one to pull him back, and I fear having to kick it away so it doesn't bite Marcel.

We've just started our walk in this quiet neighborhood of mostly single-family homes, no McMansions, a few broken-down cars, a handful of garage doors that are always open and which we suspect are broken or left open for the cats. We each have our favorite houses—the long, low green one, the yellow one with the tremendous garden, the brown one with the Christmas wreath on the door even though it's July, the two-family with the nice lady who knew Marcel from somewhere and often comes out to say hello. But we aren't there yet.

We also haven't reached the house where, a few weeks ago, the car backed out of the driveway and hit Marcel. Tapped him, really, at least in the terminology the police would use when he had the nursing home staff call them. Diminishing the incident even as they wrote it down. I couldn't imagine they'd call it a "tap" if he were a kid on a bike instead of a man in a wheelchair, but I wasn't with him when he took the police back to the house so I couldn't add the proper gravity.

The house of the man who hit Marcel with his car is white with black shutters with additions on each side. It's just around the corner, but that's no excuse. The old man in that house was sorry. So sorry. He didn't see him, he said. He didn't admit that he didn't look in his rearview, didn't look over his shoulder. He said Marcel wasn't there, and then he was, which is impossible. Marcel cannot dart out. Darting is not something he has ever done.

He hit him with his car, but he didn't run him over. To his credit, he stopped, got out, asked if he were okay. He interpreted Marcel's reaction as him being okay even though he was shaken. He said, okay, I'll leave you to it, and then he got in his car and drove away and did not make sure Marcel was steady enough to get himself back to the nursing home.

I wasn't there the day Marcel got hit by the car, but he showed me the house. I said, "At least he stopped." He shook his head. "He didn't stop?" He shook his head again, frustrated this time. I felt the tingle of anxiety I get when I sometimes misunderstand Marcel. "He stopped," I say, guessing, desperate to get it right. "But he didn't wait with you or help you get home or call for help." Marcel makes a noise between outrage and acquisition—a "yeah," with a pitch of anger. I can tell by the way he nods that I've successfully or nearly successfully articulated what he wants to say. His communication device doesn't work in the sun so today this is the best we can do.

It makes me feel useful to give Marcel my time, my attention. I also feel the particular pleasure of this friendship—that he has chosen me to be the one to help him tell the story of what happened. I don't feel this way in any other area of my life at this time, in my early thirties. All my other friendships are casual, Steve and I are dating but not living in the same state, my parents are healthy, and I'm working as a receptionist for a chiropractor, which means I answer the phones twenty times a shift and thank people for calling, but don't do what I consider meaningful work.

The man told the police he was sorry. They told him to be more careful, that it could have been a child he hit.

We can see the house of the man who hit Marcel from where this other man is coming down the path—not to his car or mailbox, but to us, apparently. He is taller than I am, but not tall. He has a gray and brown beard, longish gray hair, dirty jeans, a t-shirt. He says to Marcel, "Let me heal you."

There's not really time for us to do anything. I could yell for help. I could shout at him to go away. Marcel could give me a wide-eyed plea and probably then I'd do something. Probably then I'd tell him we aren't interested in his brand of healing. I'd likely be polite and a little wimpy. Later, I'll tell myself and Marcel that I didn't want to provoke someone who might be mentally unstable. He'll agree I made the right decision. But that's because he's a good friend and doesn't want to hurt my feelings.

Marcel doesn't move very quickly in the best of circumstances and in times like these, when he is stressed, his muscles refuse to fire at all. I could switch his chair to manual and skitter him away, but I don't because I don't think of it. I have only ever put his chair in manual in emergencies—once when the fire alarm went off at a hockey game and he was so stiff with fear he couldn't move at all, and once when I got him stuck in the sand at the beach because we both thought he had enough traction and clearance to get a little closer to the ocean and we were both wrong. On this deserted street, I stand beside Marcel like I've become a stop sign. Only I haven't, because the man with healing intentions doesn't stop.

The man puts his hands on Marcel's head and mutters something—a prayer, an incantation, a spell—and then he touches Marcel's shoulders, then Marcel's head again. Marcel stays very still except for his eyes which slide toward me. I meet his gaze. He doesn't make the noise he makes when he is angry or upset. He doesn't make any noise at all. He doesn't seem afraid as much as inconvenienced and so I relax a little. This is weird but not dangerous-weird. I worry the man might kiss Marcel because suddenly he puts his face close to his, but he doesn't. I'm so relieved that he doesn't kiss Marcel that my legs and brain go soft. "There," he says.

"Thank you," I say. And then, furious with myself, I add, "No." But he's gone by then.

What on earth am I thanking this guy for? For pretend-healing? For invading Marcel's space? For not trying to mug or kill us? Or am I just thankful he didn't touch me?

I think I'm just astonished. Plummeted into a kind of polite stupor, like the muscle rigidity that comes on with Marcel's fear.

We stand and sit in the street under the hot sun. We wait for him to get all the way inside and close the door before we exhale. We look at each other and I notice Marcel's posture is the same—hand on the joystick that controls his chair, slight lean forward with a slump to the side. He doesn't seem upset. I make a joke about how he should be all better now. How he should be able to ditch the wheelchair, get up and walk home. I feel like crying, but we laugh.

The wannabe healer could have done something much worse than put his hands on Marcel's head and muttered a few words. He could have had a knife or a gun or he could have used his hands to punch him or steal his money. What could I have done to save him? To save us both? Maybe nothing.

But also, it's not okay to just touch other people. We all know that, right?

Still, I won't give in to the idea that it's safer if Marcel stays inside the confines of the nursing home, which has been mentioned to both of us, separately, by nursing home staff. They say they can't protect him if they can't see him. They say no one else in the nursing home gets to go outside without supervision. I remind them that he does not have Alzheimer's or any other dementia, that he will not get lost, and that he understands the risk he's taking. His wheelchair battery could die and leave him stranded for hours (this has happened, which prompted the nursing home to tape a sign to the back of the chair with his name, address, and the facility's phone number). He could get caught in a sudden rain storm (this has happened, and shorted out his communication device, which meant months of him having no way to talk while it got repaired). He could hit the edge of the road and fall over (this has happened, but luckily it was in front of the nursing home and someone saw him right away.) He could get hit by a car (already happened). He could get robbed or attacked or stung by a bee. All of these are real risks, but Marcel understands them and so I say, over and over, that autonomy is part of being human. The nursing home staff and administrators grumble about liability and I remind them about human rights. They give in, although we revisit it every time something happens. Which, in the end, means he probably just doesn't tell anyone everything that happens when he's out by himself.

We continue through the streets, up the hill, down the hill. I say, "That was weird." Marcel nods.

I realize only belatedly that you could have rolled over the healing guy's foot. Or that you could have driven away. A quick turn to the side would have put him off balance, at the least. Although he likely would have stumbled along beside you, his hands on your head. And if you'd evaded, it might have made him angry. I don't ask you why you didn't try to get away because I didn't try to get you away and I'm the one with two working legs and working lungs and I didn't do anything.

The nursing home is long, low, and gray. It started out as one thing, and over the years has been added onto and onto so that it makes a jagged horseshoe. Having worked there, it's a familiar, comfortable place for me. Back inside, Marcel tells me it's happened before—the healing, the laying on of hands.

"With that same guy?" I ask.

No, he says. Other people, other places, other times, I interpret.

"People just touch you?"

Yes, he says.

I feel this viscerally, an itch in my skin, a heat. I shake my head, shake my hands. I've worked in customer service for most of my career, and people have occasionally touched me without my express consent—usually hugs, usually prefaced briefly by "Can I hug you?" followed immediately by the lunge forward. But I can back away, or push them away. I don't, but I can.

"I'm sorry," I say. "I should have told him to go away."

Marcel shakes his head and I feel a little better until I realize he's probably only saying it to make me feel better.

"I'm sorry," I say. I'm sorry I didn't tell the healing guy to back off. I'm sorry I didn't scream. I'm sorry I was afraid I couldn't protect Marcel if we made him mad and he had a weapon, or no weapon except his hands and feet and teeth. I'm sorry I didn't tell him Marcel has a right to be asked before being touched. I'm sorry I can't be with Marcel all the time. I'm sorry he has a disability that makes it impossible for him to walk or talk or feed himself and that many people see him as less than human because of it. I'm sorry they don't take the time to get to know him better. I'm sorry Marcel has carved patience like a shield.

These things happen, he says. This is just the way it is.

"Not fair," I say.

He rolls his eyes. Fairness is often the least of his concerns.

Nearly twenty-five years after the "healer" incident, I get a phone call on a sunny Thursday afternoon. It's from a number I don't recognize, but I'm in the habit of answering numbers I don't recognize because Marcel has been in the hospital more times than I can count and sometimes those numbers come up as spam.

A woman says, "I'm with Marcel." (pause) "And I need to know if he's all right."

I immediately don't like her or this conversation. Her tone is too sweet, too syrupy. "I don't know," I say. "You're with him." Is she trying to tell me he's not all right? There's no urgency in her voice, almost a giddiness, a giggly nervousness.

She says, "Well, uh, I can't tell."

Now I'm both annoyed and worried. If something really is wrong, she's doing a terrible job of communicating it. I ask where they are and she names a street near his house. He often goes out for a stroll, so that makes sense. "Is he tipped over? Passed out? Bleeding? Vomiting?"

"No," she says, drawing out the "o."

I get it, suddenly and with blinding clarity. I clear my throat. "You think he's not okay because he's disabled."

"Well," she huffs. "I wouldn't be able to sleep tonight if I didn't stop."

"Uh-huh," I say. Now I'm really annoyed. "Did you ask him if he was okay?"

"Yes," she says.

"And did he say he was okay?"

"It was—well—it's hard to understand him."

This makes me even angrier because not only can Marcel nod his head just fine, he was also able to pull up my phone number in his communication device for her, which means he probably also used his communication device to tell her he was okay. I say, "I think you're confusing disability with illness."

She repeats what I've said to her boyfriend, who huffs a laugh, then cheerily tells Marcel it was nice to meet him before hanging up on me.

The next time I see Marcel, I ask what happened when this lady called me. He gave me a funny look. I say, "You weren't expecting me to get mad, were you?"

He said no, she was just trying to be nice.

He's right, but only partly.

Once, a neighbor brought him back to the group home and told the house staff he shouldn't be out by himself. Nothing had happened, the neighbor just worried something would happen because of Marcel's disability. Once, a neighbor (maybe the same one) called the police when Marcel was out rolling around the neighborhood. The police came and determined Marcel was physically disabled but not mentally unable to decide whether or not to be outside.

I tell him what the woman caller had done was ableist—to see a person in a wheelchair and assume they need help. Which, actually, I would have been fine with if she'd stopped there. But the fact that she asked and then didn't believe his answer is misguided (at best), insensitive, and prejudicial. I couldn't just thank her and let her believe she was some kind of Good Samaritan. That kind of behavior—able-bodied people making a big deal over the disabled—is exactly what makes some disabled people feel like they don't have the right to be out in the world.

Marcel nodded in agreement. Still, he said, at least she was trying to be nice.

Later, I tell Steve that it's easy to be mad at people who are overtly anti-disabled, people who call him "retarded" or outright yell at him to get out of the way. But people acting under the umbrella of "niceness" feel more dangerous to me, more insidious. I believe she was truly trying to do a good thing. But does it matter what her intentions were? Diminishing a person's autonomy in the name of "double-checking" that they're okay is not okay.

Care and Keeping

In the United States, as part of the eugenics movement, forced sterilization of those with disabilities was ruled constitutional by the US Supreme Court in 1927 in Buck vs. Bell *and remained legal in some states until 2003. Eugenic efforts in the United States would eventually be used as models for the radical application of eugenic ideas in Nazi Germany which sterilized and euthanized persons with disabilities.*

—Emily Johnson, *AMA Journal of Ethics*

It is 2012 and Marcel has been having some trouble with his bowels, so we're at the gastroenterologist's office. The nurse leads us into an exam room and says, "Okay, just hop up on the table."

I laugh because I think she's making a joke. It's clear he can't hop. If she looked closely, or looked at him at all, she would see that his legs are completely flaccid and that he doesn't have much muscle control in his arms, either. She's looking instead at the chart, which apparently isn't very informative.

I look at Marcel and he looks back at me. We communicate with our eyes that this is a bad start.

"No hopping," I say. This isn't the first time we've been made aware that medical professionals don't read patient charts in preparation of seeing the patient. I've become adept at reciting that his primary diagnosis is cerebral palsy, he's had no heart attacks, and he's allergic to Reglan (the result is muscle spasms). Marcel knows all this but, because he speaks with a communication device and no one seems willing to wait for him to type-talk, I have become his spokesperson.

She stares at me.

"He can't hop. He can't stand. He uses a lift to transfer. Is that not in his chart?" I'm good at being bossy. I like being bossy. At twenty-one, I was hired by the nursing home where Marcel would eventually live to manage an activity staff of nine. At twenty-five, I bought a bookstore. I wasn't particularly good at either of those things, but I know how to speak up.

The nurse glances at Marcel as if I might be mistaken about his ability to hop. Then she quick-steps out of the room, shoulders up around her ears.

"She can't be mad at you," I say.

Marcel rolls his eyes. It seems like she might be mad, but it won't do her any good. Even if she held a gun to his head, he could not hop up on the exam table.

Marcel is here because he's been feeling full and his stomach is so bloated he looks eight months pregnant.

"Maybe you are," I say about the possible pregnancy. "We'll be filthy rich if you have a baby." He laughs. He gets the joke is men can't have babies and him being pregnant would be some kind of weird miracle. "You'll be rich," I amend. "I'll be a hanger-on-er." Marcel does his thing with his hand where he lifts it like he might punch me on the shoulder if he could reach, and I lean my head in so he can tap my head.

The doctor comes in to tell us she can't do the exam with him in a chair and that "someone" should have told her he needed a lift.

"Yes," I agree. "Someone should have." I feel like she's implying I should have told her or the nurse or the medical office, and maybe I should have made an extra call, just to be sure. I take a breath and try to smile kindly, as if there's been some honest mistake. "Isn't it in his chart?"

"I only look at the chart when I come in the room," she says.

We leave the exam room and wait over an hour for the van to come back for us. We talk, we people-watch. We don't dwell on the fact that Marcel still feels as bad as he felt when he got to the doctor's office and that we are no closer to knowing what's wrong.

The office reschedules his appointment. At that next appointment, the gastroenterologist does the exam with him reclining his chair back as far as it will go because they still don't have a lift, even though this time they've been given enough time to procure one. I'm not sure why they couldn't have done the exam with him reclining in his chair the first time, but we don't ask.

To protect Marcel's body privacy, I leave the room while the doctor does the exam. When she calls me back in, she recommends a colonoscopy. I ask if she has any idea what's going on and she says Marcel's getting older.

"Is it in part because of the CP?"

She says she doesn't know but, yeah, probably. She's gone before we can ask any other questions.

We're in the Emergency Room. It's two or three o'clock in the morning and Marcel is here, not for the first time this year (2015), because he's been vomiting feces. His colon has largely stopped contracting, or it's very slow in contracting, so once he's taken in more than his body can eliminate, he gets backed up. We've been friends for nearly fifteen years at this point, but these past few months have brought us the realization that something is really, significantly wrong. With that knowledge, I've stepped more fully into the role of advocate, helper, a person to count on. It's only been as I've realized his family won't be showing up to doctor's appointments, let alone middle-of-the-night hospitalizations. It's only when he asks if I can come be with him. But he does ask and I come. It isn't as hard as it sounds and I'm better at it than I thought I would be.

The colon, which is part of the large intestine, is a muscle whose job is to contract and push food through the body and then, ultimately, out. Marcel's colon has lost its elasticity, probably, the doctors say, because the palsy part of cerebral palsy affects the way muscles behave. Also, generally speaking, as we get older, our muscles lose elasticity. We could have been told this three years ago, at the first gastroenterologist's appointment, but that doctor didn't know (which I doubt) or bother. Maybe he figured knowing what was to come wouldn't do Marcel any good.

The intern who floats in to put a stethoscope to Marcel's belly and see about a CT scan says, "He's sixty-five and he has cerebral palsy? He's lucky to still be alive." She says this to me. She's very young, and I try to forgive her, but Marcel's face is folded up with grief, bottom lip over top, eyes wet with tears. He can't even grab a tissue for the sake of dignity. I yank a paper towel out of the dispenser and hold it up so he can blow his nose.

"He can hear you," I say. I say this quietly, but not so Marcel can't hear me, just quiet enough to make it clear I'm not yelling.

Marcel has resumed crying. It is a cry of frustration, but also resignation.

The intern looks at us blankly before she floats out again.

Cerebral palsy occurs at or shortly after birth, most often due to a lack of oxygen to the brain. The life expectancy of someone with CP is the same as that for anyone else, although there are various complications that are likely to shorten a person's life span if they're lucky enough not to die young.

Marcel types on his communication device. "Jennifer, I think this is maybe the—"

"End" is what he's going to say.

Instead of letting you finish, I put my thumb over the place where the laser on your glasses connects with your communication device. Essentially, this is like putting a hand over your mouth, and it's something I've never done before, but I've also never heard you come close to giving up. I don't want you to say you're ready to give up, because if you are, if you really are, I'll help you. It would be the decent thing to do. I've fought too long for your autonomy to turn away now and say you can't make your own decisions. I'll help advocate to stop treatment. If you want, I can help you fill out a Do Not Hospitalize form and the nursing home will no longer send you out. But I'm not ready for that. I love being your friend. I'm crying, too.

We're very tired. It's the middle of the night and Marcel has been vomiting feces and he's afraid and I'm afraid for him. This is the fifth or sixth time we've been in the ER in the middle of the night in just three or four months. He's had CT scans and X-rays and no one can find anything wrong and no one can help him stop vomiting feces. It's nearly impossible to vomit feces, just because of how the body is put together, which we've been told multiple times. A person's bowels would have to be incredibly backed up for that to happen, and yet that's precisely what's been happening.

Marcel doesn't yet have an ileostomy. He doesn't yet have a feeding tube. He has not yet spent three months and then five months, respectively, in the hospital. He has not yet spent Christmas in intensive care, or received Last Rites, or been told he can't return to his group home because he's too much work, medically. During this bout of bloating and vomiting, Marcel and I are sure we will come out on the other side of it—we think this is a singular medical crisis. Neither of us realize the decades of crises ahead of us.

"If only your body could surprise us in more fun ways," I say one afternoon after Marcel has vomited smelly brown poop all down his shirt. He laughs, despite everything. It's exhausting to be an anomaly, even when you've been one your whole life.

Marcel has been on the edge, and now this intern and her heartless observation has nudged him over.

I put my head on his shoulder and move my thumb off his communication device. "Say it if you need to," I say. "But I'm not giving up."

He shakes his head.

In retrospect, I wish I'd given him the space to say more about his frustration, his fear, his exhaustion. But I was afraid that if he gave up, I would lose him. And losing Marcel would mean losing a person who counted on me to show up, a person for whom I could be my best self but who, even when I wasn't, let me try again and again.

Later, while he's asleep and I'm waiting for him to be admitted to a room, I find a pen and the back of my planner and start a letter to the human resources department of this hospital. I ask if it's common practice for medical staff to express astonishment that their patients are still alive. I say it's hard enough to have a disease that makes it impossible to do so many things, but what makes it even harder are people like that intern who act like you should be grateful not to be dead. I say Marcel has been fighting to find answers and keep a positive attitude. I say it's unacceptable for someone to talk about a person as if he isn't in the room. I say they need to include training on compassion for their interns. When he wakes, I read the letter aloud to Marcel and he nods his approval. When I get home, I type and send the letter. I never hear back.

We have asked, on many occasions, to see a doctor who specializes in cerebral palsy. We've been told there aren't any in Maine. We've been told, on a few occasions, that the doctor we're talking to has or will consult with a specialist at Massachusetts General Hospital in Boston. We've never heard the results of those conversations, in part because we hardly ever see the same doctor when you're in the hospital.

I should probably do more to see about you seeing a specialist. I should contact United Cerebral Palsy or call Mass General myself. But when you're not sick, you don't want to think about being sick. And when you're sick, we're in a crisis mode of just trying to manage your symptoms.

Besides, what will a specialist tell us that's really different than what we already know? You have cerebral palsy. You're getting older than anyone expected you would get. There are complications that come with continuing to live.

We've been told cerebral palsy is a kind of rapid aging. Among the kaleidoscope of complications, Marcel's muscles will lose tone and elasticity. That includes unseen, internal muscles like the colon, bladder, and stomach. There are medical advances to help the body along—ileostomy, catheters, feeding tubes—but every time a hole is created in the body or a foreign object is inserted, the risk of infection grows.

Later in 2015, I'm in the hospital waiting room again. I have two books, pretzels, water, and cinnamon candies with me because I'm told this will be an approximately six-hour surgery to remove his colon. Steve will come later, when he gets off work. Until a few minutes ago, I was in the pre-surgery room with Marcel. Then it was time for him to be wheeled him into surgery and I kissed his forehead and told him he'd be fine.

I've just settled myself with a book when the nurse comes out to fetch me.

"What's happened?" I ask. Panic makes me want to flap my arms. "Has something happened?" I imagine Marcel died of fright, although he seemed just averagely nervous, not panicky, when I left him five minutes ago.

She leads me to the room where Marcel is positioned on his side and the anesthesiologist stands above him, behind him, so he can't see him. He's holding a needle. "I'm not really familiar with his kind of spine," the anesthesiologist says. He gestures toward the nurse. "And she isn't sure how to read his expressions. I need you to go on that side of him," he indicates the face-side of Marcel, "and tell me if it looks like he has any pain."

I stare at the anesthesiologist. I stare at the nurse. I look at Marcel. He looks back. His brow is unfurrowed. His mouth is relaxed. He trusts me so completely it scares me. The nurse and anesthesiologist look at me. The plan, apparently, is for me to stand facing Marcel while the anesthesiologist inserts a needle into his spine. If he feels pain, he will presumably make a face that I will be able to interpret as pain. Surely, they have a better method than this.

I go around the bed. I take Marcel's hand. I try to act like this is totally fine so he'll keep his misguided trust in me. "Okay, bud. So, I guess I'm gonna tell them if they hit something they aren't supposed to hit with that needle." Which is very big, although I don't say that. "So, what I need you to do is make sure you give me the most expressive face you can if you have any pain. Now is not the time to hold back. Okay?" Marcel nods. The anesthesiologist asks, "We ready?"

I look at Marcel very closely. I try to make my face as steady as possible. Marcel looks at me with trust and a tiny bit of fear. If I were him, I'd be crying my head off, but he's composed. This is not the worst thing that's ever happened to him. "He is," I say. I'm not, but I can't very well tell them that because if they say they can't do this surgery Marcel will continue to suffer. I feel like I might pass out from the anxiety of what happens if I get this wrong—how much will it hurt if he hits "something" he isn't supposed to hit? I know Marcel—I've known him for more than fifteen years at this point—but do I know the planes of his face well enough to understand a change? Will I recognize pain? I think I will. I hope I will. I'm more or less sure I will. But, will I be quick enough to speak up if there's pain or will my uncertainty cause hesitation and in turn cause him more pain?

He inserts the needle.

Marcel's face doesn't move.

"Are you okay?" I ask.

He grunts yes.

"Is he okay?" the anesthesiologist asks.

I wait a beat to make sure he isn't just saying he's okay when he's not okay. His brown eyes are as steady as solid ground. I wish he could tell me for sure that I haven't screwed this up. "He's okay," I say. And then I kiss his forehead and head back out to the waiting room.

Marcel's colon weighs twenty-two pounds when it's removed. In most people, the colon weighs four pounds. By the time the surgeon finds me and Steve in the waiting room, I've crunched through all my cinnamon candy, drunk half my water, read all my magazines twice, and checked Facebook about a thousand times. Marcel's aunt, Leta, has sent me a single message asking me to keep her posted. Neither she nor any of his cousins have come today. They haven't asked to come. They haven't asked if Marcel or I needed them to come.

The surgeon shows me and Steve a picture of Marcel's colon in a bucket. He says it's the biggest one he's ever seen. He's quite proud of this, as if it's a fish he's caught.

That night, I wait until you get to your room. I kiss your forehead and then I go home and promise I'll be back the next day, which is Halloween. You'll be back home to the nursing home by Thanksgiving, we've been told. The doctor said two weeks for your recovery, so we plan on four, knowing how things tend to go a little slower for you.

Almost immediately, you get an infection. You almost die.

When it's clear you won't die, I Facebook message members of your family and beg them to visit, mostly because I know it will cheer you up, but also so I can have a break. I'm at the hospital every day, making sure your TV is tuned to The Price Is Right *in the morning,* Dr. Phil *in the afternoon, the Bruins when they're on. I'm there when they bring in your tray, and I feed you even though no one asks me to. You can't feed yourself and I've never seen an aide come in to feed you. I ask you if they feed you when I'm not there and you say "sometimes." I suppose you wouldn't die if you missed a day of TV or even food and so I could not come if I really wanted a break. But I worry about your morale, about what it would feel like to lie in bed and want a bite of chocolate pudding and have it there, just out of reach, for hours.*

You're on soft solids at first and so I fill out your menu cards for pudding but not Jell-O, coffee with five creams and five sugars, chocolate or strawberry ice cream, macaroni and cheese, and mashed potatoes with extra gravy. I show the nurses how to set up your com-

munication device. I write instructions for your communication device as well as a list of shows you like to watch and what channels and times they are on and tape both lists to the wall with surgical tape.

Your family doesn't come. The ones who respond to my messages say they have work, families of their own. I don't tell you that I've reached out to them and you don't ask where they are. It's been so long since you've had contact with any of them that you don't expect to see them.

A priest comes and gives you Last Rites, just in case. I'm not there when it happens. You tell me the priest came and I say that's great and I ask if you prayed together and you start to cry and then you tell me he gave you—and here you say something about goodbye and dying and I say, "Last Rites?" and you say yes.

"Did he ask if you wanted them?"

With a wail, you say no.

I tell you it's just a precaution, because you're here in the hospital, but you've been Catholic longer than I have and you know that's not true. They think you're dying.

You are not ready to die.

Your infection clears, miraculously. The doctor asks me about giving you a drug that might help "move things along." It's a drug you're allergic to and you remind him of that. The doctor asks the side effects and you say "moving" which I interpret to mean spasticity but the doctor convinces you to try it because the spasms might not be that bad. You take one dose and are flailing in your bed like a fish out of water. You are so miserably uncomfortable that, for the first time ever, I can't stay with you. This is the point when I lose it. I go to my car and cry and cry and cry before I drive to work. I feel like I've failed you.

I come back, though. We're visiting when the doctor says you'd be a lot better off if you could get up and walk around. You and I start laughing, because this is an utterly ridiculous statement. You can't walk, have never in your life walked, can't even sit or roll onto your side without help.

"Did you bring your magic wand?" I ask the doctor.

The doctor doesn't laugh. He's annoyed you aren't getting better. He's annoyed because this surgery and recovery was supposed to go one way and now you with your disability have caused it to go another. He doesn't say this, but he's definitely frustrated. Maybe, in fairness, he's frustrated because he doesn't know what to do.

When he leaves the room, I say, "You should probably stop pretending you can't walk." We both crack up.

By the time you finally leave the hospital, they'll have taken down the big Christmas tree with the red velvet bows. It will be the middle of January, after all.

In November 2019, we're at the hospital for Marcel to have a feeding tube put in. He's lost sixty pounds in the past year, and the group home where he's now living has pushed hard for the feeding tube. Initially, they made it a condition of his continuing to live in the group home, but after we hired a lawyer from Disability Rights Maine, they changed their approach to a more concerned "for your health" kind of thing.

It will turn out that the weight loss is from a bowel obstruction, which seems crazy given that Marcel has about an inch of bowel attaching his ileostomy to the rest of his insides. We don't know that for a year, though, when he finally has a colonoscopy. In the year that precedes the colonoscopy, he will throw up almost every time he eats and then, rationally, he will stop eating because he's afraid to throw up. Because he can't cough very effectively (coughing requires quite a bit of muscle control), he's at high risk for aspiration pneumonia, which is the kind of pneumonia that occurs when a person inhales something (in this case, vomit) and it sits in the lungs (because he can't cough it loose) and grows into a pneumonia. Marcel has had pneumonia twice in the past year that we know of for sure, but possibly more than that. He can't always feel it, so sometimes it shows up on an X-ray and the doctor treats it with an antibiotic. Marcel could become resistant to the antibiotics at some point, which will leave the infection rampant in his already compromised immune system.

He agrees to the feeding tube when he finds out he can continue to eat by mouth with one. We're both surprised by the information. Ultimately, he decides the feeding tube will be for nutritional support. It will keep his weight steady when he cannot eat by mouth. It will take the pressure off.

The insertion of the feeding tube is planned as a day surgery, even though the group home has tried to have the hospital keep Marcel until they know he can tolerate the feedings. There's some back and forth because the group home can't support him if the tube will be pump-fed versus gravity-fed (this has to do with the level of care the group home is able to provide), but the hospital says he'll be in and out in a day and that's that.

Marcel is nervous, and so am I. It's the day before Thanksgiving. The last time he had surgery that was supposed to be easy, the ileostomy, he was in the hospital for almost three months.

We're in the room where they'll prep him and take him in for surgery. The nurse asks for his chart, and the support staff who has brought him hands it over. The nurse opens it, turns the pages, looks up. It turns out his "chart" is a folder filled with empty pages. His support staff looks baffled.

I, with as much calm as I can muster, leave the room and call the regional manager of the group home where Marcel has been living and explain that he was not sent with his chart, that he was sent with blank pages.

"That's impossible," the regional manager says.

"Unless they wrote it in invisible ink, it's all blank," I say.

I'm at the nurses' station when I call, not in Marcel's room, because I'm both furious with the incompetence of the group home and scared the hospital won't be able to perform the surgery without the necessary information and I don't want him to see how scared I am.

"How could they send a blank chart?" I ask the regional manager.

"They didn't," she says.

"It's blank," I say.

"It can't be," she says.

In the end, she faxes over what's needed and Marcel has the surgery. The procedure itself takes fifteen minutes. He feels fine. He goes home. The next day, he eats a turkey dinner by mouth.

About a week after the successful insertion of the feeding tube, Marcel is at the rehab facility because, even though the feeding tube is working fine, he lost too much strength when he got sick. At this point, he can't sit in his wheelchair for more than a couple of hours because his muscle tone is so degraded he ends up leaning way over the side, which is both painful and dangerous.

While he's in the rehab facility, he falls out of bed. It's a very slow fall, caused by a muscle spasm. His legs go first, and then their weight pulls the rest of him. Somehow he turns and falls on his face. He breaks his cheek bones on both sides and comes very close to needing surgery to keep his eyeball in place.

He couldn't ring for help before he fell because he slid away from his call bell. Marcel tells me he yelled, but the staff didn't hear him. In part, I'm sure, because his face was against the floor.

Marcel is terrified it will happen again, which I think is fair. He asks for bedrails, which seems totally reasonable to me.

The rehab facility has a policy against bedrails because they're considered restraints. "Look," I say to the nurse at the nurses' station. "I get it. My grandmother was in a nursing home in the '80s and it was terrible to see people tied to their chairs. This is not that. He's asking for bedrails to keep him from breaking his face again."

As a solution, they've lowered Marcel's bed as far as it will go and put a mat on the floor, which means if he falls again, the fall will be shorter with a softer landing.

The nurse, who is very pregnant and I'm sure exhausted, repeats, in her fake-patient voice, "Bedrails are considered a restraint."

"He can sign something," I say. "A waiver."

She's implacable.

"Okay," I say in a voice that indicates nothing is okay. "I'll go to Walmart and buy some bedrails and put them in myself and then I'll call the ombudsman and let them know you can't find a way to do this one thing so he's not anxious while he's in bed. Which is all the time."

She sighs. "Fine. I'll see if maintenance can find any."

The next day Marcel has bedrails.

In 2022, Marcel is in the hospital because he's been throwing up again (it will turn out to be another bowel obstruction) and the hospital social worker calls me. "We need permission to treat," she says.

"Is Marcel unconscious?" I ask. I'm on my way to dinner with a friend, my hand on the door, about to get out of the car, and I'm momentarily terrified that Marcel might be so sick he can't respond to questions.

"Oh, no," she says cheerfully. "He seemed quite alert when I saw him a few minutes ago."

I get out of the car, angry now because I know what she's going to say before I even ask my question. "So, why are you calling me?"

Now it's her turn to pause. "Well," she says. "I've just. . . I've never. . . you must understand that with someone who looks. . ."

I let her flounder. I know she's hoping I'll leap in and rescue her because she assumes she and I are on the same team—the able-bodied team—and she expects I can understand why she would assume a cognitive disability goes with a physical one. Which is why she didn't bother to ask Marcel if they could treat him.

I walk all the way to the restaurant door, letting her explain and backpedal. Finally, I say, "Do you have his chart in front of you?"

"Yes," she says. She sounds relieved I've given her a question she can answer.

"Then you can see he's his own guardian."

"But he can't sign anything," she says, triumphant.

This isn't really true, because he has a stamp and it's probably in his bag, but maybe it's not there or she doesn't know about it. "So, you need me to come in and sign paperwork?" I'm actually hopeful at this point, because if that's the case, this whole exchange is a little less awful.

"No," she says, although I can tell she wishes she could say yes. "I just need your verbal okay."

I wait a beat. I'm still hoping she'll fix this mess herself. "But not his verbal okay?"

She says, "I just. . . I just can't tell when he's saying yes. Can he say yes?"

He can say yes, both with his voice and with his communication device. He may not have his communication device set up, I'll give her that. And maybe she didn't understand the push of air that sounds pretty clearly to me as "yeah."

"He can nod," I say. I keep my voice level because I've learned I lose credibility when I yell.

"Oh," she says. "I didn't know that."

How long were you with him? I want to ask. *How much did you talk to him? Did you try?* But my friend has arrived at the restaurant and so I say okay and thank you and hang up and hug my friend and go inside and eat a nice dinner.

Marcel is in the hospital again because—you guessed it—bowel obstruction. I come in and put his TV on the station he likes so he can watch *Let's Make a Deal* and then *The Price Is Right.* I notice that his call bell is where he can't reach it, so I pin it to the sheet above his belly.

"Can you reach that?" I ask.

He says yes, and he's about to say more when the nurse bustles in.

"I moved the call bell," she says unpinning it from where I just pinned it. "Because he keeps hitting it by accident."

"So, you moved it to where he couldn't hit it at all?" I ask.

"We're very busy," she says.

I stare at her. She busies herself with checking his IV.

"No," I say finally. "That's really too bad that you're busy and probably short-staffed. But he's going to have this call bell where he can hit it and if he sometimes hits it by accident and you have to take thirty seconds to check on him and shut it off, that's too bad. And if I ever come in here again and find it where he can't reach it, I will let your boss know, but I will also make sure the ombudsman, Adult Protective Services, and the licensing board knows."

No way would my twenty-four-year-old self have said any of that. And even though now, at nearly forty-five, I'm trembling, at least I did it. I have, since the very earliest days of our friendship, felt like I could do almost anything for Marcel. This, I imagine, is what parents feel for their children, although I don't think of Marcel as childish. His disability gives me an opportunity for advocacy.

It feels good to say what needs to be said. Marcel lights up with the rightness of it. There have been years of these types of interactions and a kind of post-game analysis where I tell Marcel all the things I wished I'd said and he nods and tells me it's okay. And so it feels amazing to stick the landing, at last. But there's also part of Marcel and part of me that worries I've said too much and staff will be mean to him when I'm not around. It's happened before.

It doesn't happen this time. Every time I come in after that, the call bell is always pinned where he can reach it.

You are in the hospital again and this time, the social worker comes in with a DNR for you to sign. "It means Do Not Resuscitate," she explains.

We know. You've been asked to sign one every time you're admitted to the hospital. Which is often. You are nearing seventy years old, which we both know is remarkable for someone with severe cerebral palsy.

You shake your head.

"He doesn't want a DNR," I say.

The social worker blinks at me. "If he doesn't sign it, it means they'll use all the tools available to keep him alive," she says.

"We know," I say.

"Machines, tubes. . ." She sounds downright desperate.

"He understands," I say.

"Even if he's brain dead," she says to me as if you have disappeared from the room. "They'll keep him alive."

"We understand," I say.

She holds the clipboard and pen close to her chest. She's probably wondering why I don't interject, why I don't insist you sign the DNR. I don't bother explaining that I'm here to support you, not make decisions for you.

I look at you and you nod. "He wants to be alive," I say.

Do Not Resuscitate

> *Those who acknowledge a poor prognosis but still request full resuscitation may do so because they fear the consequences of a DNR order. While DNR patients felt that a DNR order would emphasize a more "natural" and comfort-oriented plan of care, FC patients felt that a DNR order would lead to passive or suboptimal care, or outright euthanasia.*
>
> — Journal of General Internal Medicine

During another hospital stay, Marcel and I had a Zoom meeting with Julie, the Palliative Care Nurse. She was in the room with him while I was at my new job with my door closed. It was late 2021, and COVID restrictions were still in place at the hospital, which was why I wasn't there with him. Also, it was my first week in my new job and I was overwhelmed and trying to make a good impression. Marcel was in bed and Julie stood beside him. He looked alert, bright, eager to hear what she had to say.

Julie said Marcel had done well for all his seventy-one years. He nodded at this, proud of himself. She allowed a pause, then she said there's a limit to what medicine can do, and Marcel may be at that limit. She was very gentle about the whole thing, but his mouth twisted open into a cry. One moment he was hopeful, the next, deflated. I hated that I wasn't there with him, just to put my hand on his. Some part of Marcel must have known this, because his body has been through so many failures these past few years. Also, he's heard what the doctors and nurses say about his prognosis (mostly that his body will continue to fail, bit by bit), as well as what they say about him when they think he can't hear or doesn't understand. I've heard it, too, but right now, with kind and calm Julie, I understood the phrase "grief-stricken."

As soon as Marcel started to cry, I started to cry.

Julie stayed admirably composed. She said he should think about the level of comfort he wanted versus the length of his life. Julie said, "Drinking, or eating, is risky for you." To her credit, she addressed Marcel. "And so, if you're asking the hospital to do everything they can to keep you alive with a Full Code* status, it's contradictory to then also ask to allow you to eat and drink."

I interrupted her. "But people are Full Code and do lots of things that could be risky—they scuba drive and climb mountains and smoke cigarettes."

I was outraged, but Julie met my outrage with calm. "Certainly," she said.

She was very nice.

* According to The Ohio State University, "Full code means that if a person's heart stopped beating and/or they stopped breathing, all resuscitation procedures will be provided to keep them alive. This process can include chest compressions, intubation and defibrillation, and is referred to as CPR. This is the default code status for all patients unless they have had an explicit conversation with their medical provider to indicate otherwise."

Marcel hasn't been eating or drinking anything by mouth because the most recent test done at the hospital suggested his aspiration risk has increased. Aspiration means inhaling food into the lungs instead of swallowing it, which means a higher risk of food sitting in his lungs and potentially causing pneumonia. Pneumonia could be fatal for him at this point in his life. He's always been an aspiration risk, which I point out to anyone who will listen, but they keep telling me it's gotten worse and who am I to say it hasn't? When I asked, Marcel said maybe, maybe his swallowing has felt stranger, more difficult. It was hard to tell.

Julie asked only that he think about his Full Code status, and that he and I continue to have these conversations.

Later that week, when I visited in person, Marcel told me he believed not being a Full Code, in essence not asking the doctors to do everything they could to keep him alive, was the same as giving up. It's the same, he feels, as a kind of passive suicide.

In all the years I'd known Marcel, I had worked remarkably hard to not talk to him about death. In the early years of our friendship, I was working on a print documentary of Marcel for a graduate class. It was then he told me about his brother, about his suicide. What Marcel said at the time was that his brother died of depression. I didn't know what to say to that. In the intervening years, we've talked about it from time to time, but always obliquely. Not because I can't handle Marcel's sadness, but because there's nothing actionable I can do. I can't bring George back. I *can* just listen, though, and I'm trying to be better about leaving space for that.

And now here he was, taking it even further, saying that suicide was not just about an active death but a passive giving up, too. Marcel was pushing hard to live, no matter what.

"I don't think that's true, though," I said. "I don't think allowing nature to take its course is the same as killing yourself."

Marcel was not convinced.

On my way out, I stopped by the nurses' station and relayed the conversation to Julie. I asked her to have the hospital chaplain stop by in the hope that he might reinforce what I said. Not that I wanted Marcel to give up, but I wanted him to know he could.

The second time Julie met with us was in person. She reminded us we should think of aging with a chronic illness as a kind of rapid aging.

"It's the one thing you can do fast," I said and Marcel rolled his eyes and then laughed.

Julie, in her soft, velvety voice, explained that a Full Code meant the doctors and nurses would try to bring him back to life after he'd died. Which means after his heart stopped. We were in Marcel's hospital room. He was in bed, and I wished he wasn't because he looks less like himself when he's in bed. He looks more diminished, less vital, and that's not the Marcel I wanted Julie to see. I wanted her to believe—like I believed—that if he died and was brought back, he would be the man who laughs at my jokes and wants to go out on cold winter nights to look at Christmas lights and who will go with me to pet goats even though he hates the smell of farm animals. He will be the him who I can't wait to tell what I bought my husband for Christmas, who asks me to help spell a name to put in his communication device, who teases me when I cry through every single movie we've ever watched together.

Julie explained that the chances of a doctor successfully bringing anyone over the age of seventy back to full "before" status is very slim. The chances are even slimmer because of the cerebral palsy. My whole body buzzed with a kind of disbelief—not that Marcel would or could die—but this, this feels like being asked to give up hope, to concede defeat. I held his hand.

I said, "What Julie told me on the phone is that what she means isn't that they would be unsuccessful and you would die, but that you'd come back as a vegetable." I hated saying this. I hated myself for saying this. I didn't want it to be true and even if it was true, I didn't want it.

Julie nodded. "That's right," she said. "You wouldn't come back the way you are now."

Marcel looked up at the ceiling. He stopped crying. I didn't think he was praying. I thought he was just taking a moment to gather his thoughts.

"You don't have to decide anything right now," I said. In the months and years that follow this conversation, I will say how grateful I am to Julie for being the person who finally lays it out for us. The person who finally explains to us what being Full Code really looks like. But at this moment, I was not grateful. I was just sad that he was being asked to give up yet another thing.

I said, "This doesn't mean they won't treat you if you get sick."

"Right," Julie said. "This would come into play only if your heart stops."

"Which it never has," I said. "In all these years, Marcel, you've never had to have anyone bring you back to life." Still, I thought it must be nice to know the option was there—to die and come back.

"And it isn't the same as giving up," I said. Marcel and I were both raised with the Catholic belief that doing anything less than everything possible—every medical treatment, every intervention—is the same as slow suicide. That life—no matter what that looks like—cannot be willfully given up. It's an idea I struggle to let go of even now, when I hear about a friends' parents who, rather than aging poorly, committed suicide together. I want to admire them for choosing their own path, and yet what I feel is a kind of dread.

Marcel looked at me, then at Julie, and nodded.

I said, “We aren’t going to interpret what you’re saying. It’s too important.” I gestured for him to type into his communication device.

He typed and then spoke: “I want DNR.”

I should have felt relieved, but I suspected he agreed to the DNR not because he believed it was the best thing but because he wanted to eat and drink while in the hospital.

And I was right, because the next time he’s in the hospital, he doesn’t sign the DNR.

And I don’t try to have the conversation with him again. I tell myself that if he wants to talk about it, he knows I’m here to listen.

Let's (Not) Talk About Sex

> *We are denying people (with disabilities) a fundamental part of being human—the right to have intimacy and connectedness. We do this because it makes us uncomfortable, without ever asking what's right for them.*
>
> —Nancy Fitzsimons, *Star Tribune*

I'm in graduate school for documentary studies and you're my subject. At one of our interview sessions, I get the tape recorder set up and then I ask you if you have any disappointments in life. It's kind of a stupid question, because I already know you can't walk or talk, you've been to school only briefly as an adult, and you can't read, which is something you're working on. But I've been told by my teachers in this program that I should open with general questions. We're in your room in the nursing home. You're too young to be in a nursing home—forty-nine—but you have cerebral palsy and so here you are. Your roommate keeps opening and closing the door. The nurses' aid keeps taking the door out of his hand and pressing it open against the huge magnet that holds the door in place. "This needs to stay open," she says sternly to your roommate. I don't know this roommate's name. They die so often I've stopped bothering to learn names.

You type into your communication device that you wish you'd had a family.

I say, "You mean you wish your family came to see you more often?" I want to believe it's not because you're disabled that I don't immediately understand what you mean by having a family, but I'm not sure that's true.

"No," you type. "Kids."

"You wanted kids?" I'm surprised, and I don't keep the surprise out of my voice.

"Yes," you type. "And a wife."

"That's great," I say, which is inane. And then I inexpertly pivot the conversation and ask what you like to eat.

What I should have asked was if you'd ever dated, if you'd ever fallen in love, if there were particular barriers to the physical act of sex. I think now of Christopher Reeve who, after his spinal cord injury, continued to have sex with his wife, albeit in an altered way. I could have used Reeve's experience to get us talking about what sex might look like for you. But I have never been comfortable talking about sex, and so I didn't.

I wouldn't have wanted to talk about sex with anyone, no matter what they looked like. But it's also true that I was upset by you wanting things you probably couldn't have or couldn't have easily. Or that I didn't think you could have. I was uncomfortable with the fact that I couldn't fix your disability and, by extension, couldn't fix this part of your life.

We're visiting your Aunt Leta in her apartment. After her husband Gil, your mother's brother, died in 2008, she moved to this apartment. A few weeks prior, you asked me to call her and arrange a visit and so she and I picked a date and I reserved the handicapped van and I drove you to the apartment and she buzzed us in. She tells us, by way of explaining why she hasn't visited you, that it's hard for her to get around these days. She says this with no irony, even though you are, and have always been, in a wheelchair.

I don't know what we're talking about when Leta launches into a story. "I'm sorry," Leta says. "I probably shouldn't be telling you this." Her whole body trembles with laughter, her face is lit with delight. She reminds me of Mrs. Claus. "You know, the nurse has to give you a hard-on in order to insert a catheter."

I didn't know, but then I hadn't ever considered the catheterization process at all. You and I have been friends for a decade now, but still, we never talk about sex or parts of the body related to sex.

Leta's apartment is small and cluttered with ceramic dolls painted with huge eyes and tremendous lashes. The dolls cluster every surface—the top of the TV, both sides of the TV stand, the small half wall that separates the kitchen from the living room, the window sill. This is only the third or fourth time I've met Leta. The first was when your Uncle Gil was in the hospital. The second was at his wake.

She says, "He got a pretty nurse and she's just holding his penis and he's loving it."

You let out a groan of embarrassment and I feel the heat rise to my cheeks. I stare at the gold cross nestled in the folds of Leta's ample cleavage.

Leta says, "I told him not to be embarrassed—that any guy would get hard with a pretty girl holding his penis. He should be proud that God gave him such a beautiful penis. He should be glad it works."

You and I studiously do not look at each other. I don't want to think about your penis and I'm sure you don't want me to think about your penis. We have never talked about sex. I don't talk about sex with anyone, which is what I would say in defense of myself, but the truth is I've never thought of you as someone who might have sexual feelings.

I have definitely never entertained the thought that you might have those kinds of feelings for me, but now, with Leta pointedly telling this story, I wonder if she thinks you think of me that way. I stop myself from wondering by squeezing my hands into fists and allowing my nails to pierce my palms.

Leta says, "Nothing else on his body works, but he has that beautiful penis."

I laugh, mostly as a distraction. Also, maybe a kind of punctuation. I'm hoping Leta will understand it's time to change the subject.

She says, "The nurse has to rub it a little, you know."

I didn't know. I point at one of the ceramic dolls. "Did you paint this?"

"Oh, no," Leta says. She seems equally delighted to talk about ceramics as she did to talk about your penis. "My hand is too unsteady. My neighbor makes them. Aren't they something?"

They're creepy, in fact, all lined up all over the place with their innocent eyes and painted overalls and smock dresses. Like a school of inert kindergarteners. But I'm thrilled to have moved the conversation to inanimate objects and, beside me, I feel you relax, too.

Finally, it's time to go and we make our way down the hall, down the elevator, into the van. I chatter away about the dolls, how creepy that were, did you think they were creepy?

Neither of us ever says anything about the penis conversation.

Until I was ten, I thought people had to be married in order to have sex. Meaning that, once you received the Sacrament of Marriage, God gave you the parts necessary to do the sex act. I was not entirely sure what that entailed, and I would stay unsure until I was nearly thirteen, when a girl I hardly knew drew me a diagram.

But this isn't only about me being uncomfortable with sex. It's about my maternal role in our relationship that borders on me infantilizing you. About me thinking of you as an object of my affection that is a full stop at platonic. I could stretch this metaphor to those creepy dolls if I wanted to.

I'm glad our friendship has never been complicated by the undercurrent of sex, but I'm sorry I didn't hold space for you to talk about it more. It's possible, though, that you said all you wanted to say to me about sex—that you wished you'd had the chance to love someone in that way. I wish it for you, too. You would have made someone an excellent partner. Maybe we could have talked about sex more, but maybe we're just the kind of people who like to keep private things private.

Marcel's friend Jack has cerebral palsy, too. In the early 2000s, when they're both in the nursing home, one of the nurses tells me Jack has filed a complaint with the state because the nursing staff refuses to masturbate him while he watches porn. Jack is in his mid-thirties and, were he not disabled, he would absolutely be the kind of guy catcalling women.

I'm sure Jack told Marcel about his complaint. But I never ask Marcel what he thinks and I never hear what happens.

I express sympathy to the staff, but privately I think Jack is kind of amazing to advocate for himself and his needs. I don't think this is something nurses should have to do, but I think it's great that he wants them to. And yet I blush wildly when I try to tell my husband what the nurse told me.

To my husband, I say, "Sex is a part of being human and just because someone is disabled doesn't make that desire go away."

He agrees. "But that doesn't seem like it should be the job of the nursing staff," he says.

Years later, Jack will get a girlfriend. He meets her through a group called Speaking Up for Us. She has obvious cognitive impairments and, yet, they spend hours alone in Jack's room. Marcel watches with envy when he sees them together, her kissing his forehead before her ride comes to pick her up.

Marcel tells me once that he doesn't think Jack is very nice to his girlfriend. I ask what makes him think that but he just shrugs.

"Jack isn't nice to anyone," I say.

Marcel agrees.

"You think he's taking advantage of her?" I ask.

Marcel nods.

And, yet, there's something about Jack that Marcel admires. He seems to care not at all about his disability, which is in many ways more profound than Marcel's. He seems angry about it, emboldened by it. He uses it to his advantage in a way neither of us can quite figure out, but that is, for lack of a better word, attractive.

When I'm eleven or twelve, my friends and I are squished into the booth that is our kitchen table. We are playing Truth or Dare, but really just Truth. My mom comes in and slides into the booth next to me. My mom is pretty and fun and all my friends love her. The friend sitting across from me is my wild friend, also named Jen, who will be the first among us to have casual sex in college.

Maybe I feel emboldened by Jen's presence, but when it's my mother's turn to answer a Truth, I pull the neck of my t-shirt up over my mouth, lean in to her ear, and whisper, "How many times have you and Daddy done it?"

My mother rears back as if I've spit on her. "That's private," she says. "I'm surprised at you."

I want to cry, but I'm known for crying and so I hold back long enough to get to the bathroom and run the tap. When I come back out, my mother has gotten up to unload the dishwasher.

When you're in the group home, one of the male staff asks Steve if I give you oral sex when we're alone in your room. It's appalling that a man would ask another man if his wife is performing a sex act on a third man, but the staff person asks it casually, as if this is a perfectly normal thing to ask. He says all the staff wonders why I come to see you so much and why we keep the door closed. He says he just thought we should know what people are saying.

I don't know exactly what Steve says, but I'm sure it's kinder than "Fuck off."

When Steve tells me this, I go apoplectic with rage. "Have they never had a friend before?" I ask. "We keep the door closed because his housemate just walks in and jabbers and we can't get him to leave." I pace the room. "I should call Adult Protective Services. They have no right to say those things."

My embarrassment makes me angrier and angrier.

Steve knows the nature of our friendship and he isn't telling me what the staff person said out of anything but shock and sadness. "They haven't said it to him," he says reasonably. "I'm not sure what your complaint to Adult Protective Services would be."

"It's disgusting," I say. "We're friends!"

Neither of us ever tell you what that staff person told us. Neither of us mention it to each other ever again, either, until I write this scene in this book and I tell you and you sigh. It's disappointing, it seems, but not surprising.

Prior to the 1930s, Maine's marriage laws prohibited "idiots," "feeble-minded," and "imbeciles" from getting married because, the argument went, they couldn't understand the contract they were entering into. Between 1925 and 1963, as part of the eugenics movement, 326 Maine residents underwent forced sterilizations; 72 percent of them were considered feeble-minded.

Marcel was born in 1950 and, even though he has no cognitive impairment, his physical disability is usually enough for people to assume feeble-mindedness.

I did my documentary project in 1999, less than two years after I met Marcel. When I thumb through the transcribed pages I've kept all these years, I notice I ask him surface questions about the camp he attends, if he's gone to school, where he grew up. We touch on a few topics of more substance—his brother's suicide, his mother's overprotectiveness and fear, his family and their unwillingness to visit him. Every time we get near something serious, I laugh nervously and change the subject.

I was only twenty-four.

It was our last interview session when I asked, "What kinds of things would you look for in a girlfriend?"

Marcel said, "That she be nice and a little outgoing."

Right after he says that, a group of little kids walks past us and I comment on how cute they are, how noisy they are. I ask what he thinks of them. I say we're in a noisy location. I ask if Marcel thinks we should move. He shakes his head no to all of it. It's so obvious I'm uncomfortable with my own question about a made-up girlfriend that I feel bad for myself across all these years.

Finally, I get back around to asking if there's been anyone Marcel is interested in, maybe someone he's met at camp.

He says yes, and I clap with delight. Oh, former self.

He makes a face.

"What?" I ask. "Do you not see a possible future with her?"

He shakes his head. He says, "I can't talk." He means he talks through a communication device and that it's slow, that "normal" conversation is nearly impossible, that there are always long pauses while he types with the laser that's attached to his glasses.

I get all up on my soap box instead of really listening. I say, "That's not a good reason!" I say, "You just have to meet the right person!" And, "You can talk, you just use a computer." I don't ask what he means. I don't ask why he thinks that's a barrier. I don't ask if it would be a barrier for him if he met someone who also used a communication device. I don't ask if he's ashamed of his disability. I don't ask if he thinks people equate not talking with being "feeble-minded." I assume a lot of the answers. Now, I'm ashamed of those assumptions.

And then the tape runs out and when I turn it over, I say, "So, if you were all done talking about that, we can move on."

He says "Yeh" and I let that be the final word.

In the years since 1999, we've had deeper and more meaningful conversations about friendship and family and death and loss and fear and abandonment. We've had many serious talks about what he wants his life to look like. We've visited his parents' graves, his brother's grave. We've talked about all manner of physical ailments, including the color of his vomit and the size and weight of his colon when it's removed.

We've never talked about his desire for a family again. We've never talked about sex again.

Perhaps it's because of the more maternal nature of our relationship. Or, it's because I worry, on some level, that he doesn't see our relationship as purely maternal. That he's felt things for me I haven't felt for him and those feelings have caused him pain or disappointment. I could never have the unrequited love conversation with anyone, but especially not him. Because I couldn't stand to know I'd hurt him, especially if I'd hurt him by trying to be kind.

Or perhaps we've never talked about sex because of my prudishness. Or his prudishness—after all, he's never brought it up, either. And he was raised like me, that sex is private, not to be discussed. I'm not sure that line of thinking has benefited either of us.

But, maybe there's also something more sinister in my reluctance to talk about sex with you. Even me, who loves you, who adores you, sometimes sees you as childlike, as incapable of wanting more than you have. In some ways, this is self-protective—it's too sad to think about the life you've been denied. I imagine your reluctance to talk about sex is also, in some ways, the same kind of self-protection. But in the end what it feels like is that I have failed to acknowledge part of your humanity.

Home Sweet Home

The first Plaintiffs in a class-action lawsuit against the Maine Department of Health and Human Services (DHHS) will move from their nursing facilities into their own apartments in Bangor early next week. . . Under a settlement agreement approved by the federal court in May 2012, the state agreed to create a new home and community-based waiver program to allow those who formerly had no choice other than to live in nursing facilities to live in the community and still receive services they need.

—National Health Law Program

It was 2016, a month out from when Marcel was finally going to move from the nursing home, where he lived for nearly twenty years, into the group home. It had been four years of planning, of waiting for a spot to open up, of ordering a custom-made manual wheelchair and a portable lift. Of getting Marcel a new primary care doctor. Of making sure the group home staff will be able to take care of his new ileostomy. We'd been working with the house manager, the regional director, Marcel's case manager, and the State's ombudsman.

Marcel was nervous because change is always hard, but excited because this change meant he'd have more control of his finances, more disposable income, more privacy, and the opportunity to get out in the community more often. He might even be able to find work or a volunteer opportunity. He'd have his own bedroom (one of four), two shared bathrooms, and a community kitchen/dining area and living room. It would be much smaller than the nursing home and, hopefully, something resembling a home.

And then, at this meeting, there was a new house manager. The one we'd been working with, the one we'd liked so much, left and in her place is a woman we'll call Big M, whom we've met before and whom we did not like. When we last met her, she was staff for a woman who lived on her own, and when we visited to see if Marcel, too, might be able to live in his own apartment, Big M spoke to the woman in a sing-song voice that made our skin itch. Later, we heard Big M left that position under suspicion she'd been stealing from the woman.

There in the conference room, we looked at each other. Big M did not acknowledge she remembered us. We knew she knew us, so it was extra weird that she pretended otherwise. We thought maybe she didn't want us to remember her. We didn't call her out on it, though, because what good would that have done? We were still afraid this whole move might fall through.

Later, we talked about whether Marcel should still move, given this change in managers. He still wanted to go, in part because there had already been so much work that had gone into preparing for the move. But, also, because if he didn't go now, who knew when there would be another opening. And, how bad could it be?

It turned out that it was terrible. Big M was worse than we anticipated. It wasn't just a sing-song voice, although she used it on Marcel whenever anyone else was around.

A few months after he moved, Marcel, his case manager, the house manager, the regional manager, and I met in a big conference room at a place that wasn't the group home because Marcel didn't feel comfortable talking about what was going on at the house where staff might hear. He had been crying. He typed into his communication device that he thought he'd be allowed some say in menu planning. Part of the appeal of moving was that he'd have choices, and food choices are a big one for him (for anyone, really).

Big M said, "Well, we can't just whip up whatever you want." She said this with a huge smile, as if everyone in the room would see how unreasonable Marcel was being to want what he wanted for dinner.

Marcel's case manager asked if everyone sits down together to plan menus for the week or month.

"Yes," Big M said.

"No," Marcel said.

Big M's smile faltered. "Well," she said, "We have to meet nutritional standards. They can't just have whatever they want."

"So, they don't help plan the menu?" I asked.

She shrugged.

"No," Marcel said again.

"Even though you said they would?" I was staring at her in absolute disbelief. She wasn't even a little ashamed of herself.

She shrugged again.

We went round and round a few times about how group home staff weren't doing what they said they'd do, but eventually Marcel's case manager brought us back to what he wanted to talk about, specifically.

The particular incident he wanted to talk about that day is that he asked for a frozen meal he had purchased to be heated for his dinner instead of what was on the menu. The two staff people who were there said, "This isn't a restaurant" and then proceeded to laugh and serve him the meal he did not want, which he ate because he was hungry.

After Marcel recounted this, Big M said nothing. Her boss, who reminded me of a troll doll because her hair was styled with big, soft spikes, said, "If that really happened, they'll be spoken to. Disciplined."

"If it really happened?" I repeated, just to be sure I understood her.

She flushed. "I'll talk to them," she said.

Marcel made a noise that I understood to be fear.

In the past, when he's said something negative about house staff, they've retaliated by not answering his call bell, which meant he risked his ileostomy bag exploding. Which meant he ended up with poop all over his stomach, clothes, and dribbling onto his chair and the floor. It could also mean they don't answer his call bell when he needs to pee, in which case he either holds it and risks a urinary tract infection or he wets himself. Or, he could be ringing his call bell because he's about to be sick, is uncomfortable, would like a drink of water, wants to go to bed, or needs help making a phone call. They could fail to charge his communication device or his wheelchair, they could leave him in bed, they could threaten him with physical harm. They could physically harm him.

"Are you going to say it was Marcel who reported them?" I ask.

"No," she said. "Of course not." But I got the feeling she hasn't, until now, thought this through.

She said, "If I ever hear of anyone taking anything out on you. . ." she trailed off. To her credit, she seemed genuinely distressed. Still, I needed a plan, not just hope.

"You'll what?" I asked.

"They'll be fired," she said.

Eventually, the two who refused to make Marcel a frozen meal were fired. Not for that particular incident but not long afterwards. In the intervening weeks, I asked Marcel every time I saw him if they were treating him okay and he told me they were. But he might not tell me if they weren't. Because there was no place other than back to the nursing home for him to go and he won't go there. So, he always says everything's fine and I say I believe him and we are both so relieved when they're fired it's clear we've been lying.

Marcel loves Christmas. He especially loves Christmas lights and Christmas music. The first year he was at the group home, I asked and asked for staff to take him out to look at Christmas lights, but they never did. "Short-staffed" was the reason I was given every single time.

How much staff does it take to load a few people into a van and drive around?

The year after he moved in, I got clever. I asked to meet house staff in Marcel's old neighborhood. We can't ride in the van with him—I don't know why that's a rule, something to do with insurance—so he and they will follow us as we drive around and look at the Christmas lights. Back when Marcel lived in the nursing home, we took him around this area to look at lights so we know where all the good houses are.

We were supposed to meet at 4:30 p.m. at Sam's, a sub shop/pizza place Marcel loves, have an early dinner, then head out. The place we've chosen is halfway between Marcel's house and our house. We got there at 4:20 p.m. Forty minutes later, I called the house and the woman who answered the phone said that she didn't know who was bringing Marcel but he was not there so she guessed he left. She didn't know when he left. At 5:15 p.m., I texted Big M and the regional manager. At 5:30 p.m., I got a response from the regional manager that the staff person was lost.

"Why didn't she call me?" I asked.

The regional manager didn't know. She also didn't know why the house staff didn't know when Marcel left or who he was with. I guessed they knew, or could have found out, but just didn't care to get me an answer.

Marcel and his house staff—May—showed up at 6:30. He was flustered and upset. She said, "We only have twenty minutes, because I have to get back at the house."

"Twenty minutes to eat and see the lights?"

"I don't make the schedule," she said, unironically.

When I asked why she was so late, she said she didn't know where she was going. She didn't have GPS. She didn't think to use Google Maps before she left. It didn't occur to her to call me. Later, Marcel will tell me he didn't leave the house until nearly 6 even though he tried to tell them he was supposed to meet us at 4:30. They pretended they didn't understand, even when he typed it into his communication device instead of trying to tell them with his voice.

Marcel said he wanted to eat anyway, so we went into the sub shop and he got a sub and May fed him, and Steve and I picked at our food because we didn't feel like eating but we didn't want Marcel to be upset that we're upset. When we finished eating, I asked if we could at least go see one house and May reluctantly agreed. "I don't have much time," she said, as if this was all somehow our fault. Marcel was visibly upset—face creased, arm rigid—but I didn't ask if he'd rather just go home because I wanted him to at least get to see one Christmas-y house and if I asked, he'd say they should go, because he wouldn't want May angrier than she already was.

We got to the house that, if you tuned your radio to a certain station, you could hear music timed with the lights. We drove past the house, then turned around and May followed. We parked opposite the house for five minutes and then May texted me to say they had to go. We led her to the highway and blinked our lights goodbye.

That night, I sent an email to Big M asking why this happened and a few days later, I got an email back saying she didn't know, she'd look into it, these things happen. I cc'd the regional manager and her boss, too, but I got no response from them. I never got that follow-up email.

Marcel told us later he was glad he got to see the Christmas-y house.

Part of the problem, we will learn after years and years of this kind of behavior, is that the group home pays staff minimum wage and keeps their hours low enough that staff doesn't qualify for any kind of benefits. Which results in undermotivated staff and high turnover. Conversely, because they're chronically short-staffed, the group home management is reluctant to discipline anyone for fear they'll quit. A warm body is better than no body at all, I guess.

Another year went by, and arranging outings was no easier. It took multiple emails and months of planning, but finally we arranged for someone to bring Marcel from the group home to my parents' house for a barbeque.

It was two hours past the time he was supposed to be there. My mother was wild with nerves, but Steve and I were used to the lateness by then. We'd wisely not put the steaks on the grill yet. I called the house and the person who answered said Marcel and his staff person left and that they "should be" on the way.

When he arrived, two-and-a-half hours past the time he was supposed to be there, it was with Pam, who has a frantic, bug-eyed energy. In one breath, she said she's late because she could only go back roads because Big M wouldn't give her the E-ZPass for the toll highway and she didn't have any cash and it took her way longer than she expected and it isn't her fault. She shifted her eyes all over the place, wavered on her feet, and I could feel everyone—me, my parents, Marcel, Steve—getting agitated. Was she high? She seemed high or on the verge of a mental breakdown and I was hoping for high because she'd eventually be not-high.

My mother, ever the hostess, asked who wanted what to drink and I went inside to help her with root beer and water and seltzer. When we were out of earshot of everyone, she asked if Pam was "on something." I shook my head, although I was already planning how I'd have to get her to let me drive her and Marcel home.

We had steak and potato salad and watermelon, which Marcel likes sprinkled with salt and which my father made a big show of finding disgusting. Marcel insisted it's good, and so I tried a piece and it wasn't bad and my father made a face and Marcel laughed. Throughout the meal, Pam ate nothing. She talked instead. She told us she used to work for the group home before but got fired because another client at a different group home didn't like that she was talking about the guns she had at home. As if she'd come to work and shoot someone! She's still not allowed to work with Marcel's housemate because he's afraid of her. But, she assured us, she and Marcel got along great. Marcel wasn't worried she'd shoot him in his sleep!

She told us about her possessive ex-husband, her faulty gallbladder, the wrist surgery she couldn't afford and the subsequent pain she's in, her semi-controlled diabetes, and her very young boyfriend.

She told us she worked eighteen- to twenty-hour days without sleeping.

We all listened to Pam in a kind of stupor.

I asked Marcel if he wanted to go for a walk while Mom and Steve clean up. When Pam started to get up to join us, I insisted she stay and rest. She sat back in the chair and kept right on talking to my father. When we're on the street, I asked Marcel if he felt safe with Pam. I was prepared to find him another way home. But he said "yes."

"You feel safe?" I asked again, to confirm, and also because I didn't believe him.

He said "yes" again.

I said, "She seems kind of. . . odd."

Marcel shrugged, which did nothing to make me feel better.

"This is just the way she is?" I guessed.

He nodded.

When it was time for them to leave, I gave Pam money for tolls so she could take the highway home. I called an hour and a half after they left to make sure they got home safely, which they did.

The next day, I emailed Big M and the regional director. I told them the day was really strange. I told them the things Pam told us, unprompted, about work and her personal life. I didn't say I worried she was on drugs. They emailed me back with apologies and assurances there would be more and better staff training, but the emails seemed a bit rote. I tried not to worry.

Pam brought Marcel to several more outings and then we didn't see her again.

I worried that I'd done the wrong thing because, as unstable as she seemed, she also seemed to genuinely like and care about Marcel. I asked him if he's upset that she's gone. He shook his head a vigorous no.

We were gathered for Marcel's monthly team meeting, although "team" is a misleading moniker—these meetings felt increasingly oppositional with me, Marcel, and his case manager on one side and the house manager and regional manager on the other side. My stomach felt like boiling soup and I could see the rigidity in Marcel's body that indicated he was stressed, too.

Marcel had a message ready in his communication device. It said May wouldn't let him watch TV in the living room at night. She said nighttime is her time to watch TV and Marcel didn't think that was right.

Big M laughed. She said, in her baby-placating voice, that Marcel must have misunderstood, that May would never say that. Big M explained, as if it wasn't the very basis of his compliant, that the TV in the living room is for Marcel and the other residents. And that staff isn't paid to watch TV. She said this as if Marcel has suggested May should watch TV in the living room at night.

Marcel repeated the message he had in his communication device, restating that May watches TV in the living room at night. She says nighttime is her time to watch TV and Marcel doesn't think that's right.

Marcel's case manager said, "It sounds like this is something that's already happening."

"I'll talk to her about it," Big M said in a tone that suggested she didn't believe Marcel and likely wouldn't say anything at all to May.

Marcel told me later that May and Big M were friends, that he'd already gone to Big M with this complaint and she told him to stay in his room and watch his own TV, which he would, except some of the shows he likes aren't on the cable package he gets in his room.

I sent an email to the regional manager, her boss, and the State's ombudsman. Shortly afterward, Marcel told me he was now allowed to watch TV in the living room at night, but that May had not been fired and that, sometimes, he heard her and Big M laughing about him.

I hated them in a way that makes me feel like I could hurt them.

It was not a huge surprise when Big M got fired, but it was a relief. A week or two after Marissa started as the new house manager, Steve and I were supposed to meet Marcel at Fast Eddie's, which is about an hour and a half from our house and twenty minutes from his house. An hour before we were supposed to meet, when we were already on the road, staff called my cell and said they couldn't make it because they'd had a call out and there wasn't enough staff to bring Marcel anywhere. We were disappointed, but we brought him takeout and hung out in his room.

We ignored the fact that two staff members were outside smoking when we got there. "Everyone deserves a break," I said to Steve once we were inside. It did seem like with two staff and four people living the house, someone could have dropped Marcel off and picked him up at Fast Eddie's, but we tried to believe we didn't have all the facts.

A week later, it happened again. This time, we'd brought my parents with us because they hadn't seen Marcel in ages. The house staff called when we were almost at Fast Eddie's to say they had a call out and they wouldn't be able to bring him to Fast Eddie's. "No," I said. "You'll have to figure something out." My heart was thunder in my ears. I thought for sure they'd say no. When they hung up on me, I assumed they just wouldn't show up. I'm not proud of my fury—then or now. I'd prefer some kind of reasonable negotiation—maybe they needed an extra hour to find staff to come in, or maybe they could bring all the residents to Fast Eddie's and we could eat together. But, when it seemed like Marcel's social life was inconsequential to them, my temper flared.

I texted Marissa and her boss, Stan, the new regional manager. A few minutes later, I got a call from staff that Marcel would indeed get a ride.

The woman who brought him was livid. Her hair was long and black and wild and her movements getting him out of the van were fast and jerky. I thanked her and she glared at me. My temper turned tail and ran. I was afraid I'd done a bad thing by insisting on this outing.

I wedged a smile between my cheeks as I said, "Should I call the house when he's ready for a pickup?" This was how we'd always handled Marcel's pickup and I probably didn't need to ask, but I felt like I needed to say something to break the tension.

She threw up her hands. "I'm not even supposed to be here today. I got a call that this," she waved at Fast Eddie's as if the 1950s-style diner was to blame for all her troubles, "had to happen."

"So, we'll call the house?" I said again, because I wasn't sure what else to say. Marcel's face was all lines on his forehead and tears in his eyes. I put my hand on his back.

"I have no idea," she said. "Maybe he'll stay here all night." She nearly spit the words at us. And then she got in the van and drove away.

Marcel let out a wail. It was, I think, a wail of fear that she'd leave him here all night, fear that she'd be mean to him at some other point in time, and anger that she treated us this way. Both fear and anger pricked every nerve along my spine. They had to come back. No one had the right to talk to him like that. She had no right to make him afraid. They had to come back. I rubbed a circle on his back, which is what my father used to do for me when I had trouble sleeping. From where they stood a few feet away, my parents looked like they might run after the van. "We'll get you home," I said. I smiled at my parents and Steve and the dog, all of whom were here to see Marcel and have hamburgers and ice cream. "It's going to be fine."

As we walked across the parking lot I said, "This wouldn't be the worst place to stay. They have really good shakes." Marcel laughed, even though I knew he was nervous. Even if staff did come to pick him up, which they would because they had to, they won't be happy about it. In the future, they might not check on him. They might not put his TV on the channel he wants to watch. They might forget to charge his communication device or his wheelchair, leaving Marcel unable to talk or get around.

I texted Marissa and Stan and told them what just happened. I asked for assurances that Marcel would be picked up and that there would be no retribution in any way toward him. They texted me back rote reassurances that in no way expressed shock or outrage.

All I could do was hope they made sure he was safe. They knew I was paying attention.

I called the house when we were done eating and Marcel got picked up by a different staff person. It took her nearly an hour to get there, but she was very, very nice when she arrived. She was nice when she loaded him into the van, nice when she strapped him in.

I asked you the next time I saw you if anything bad happened as a result of that outing and you said no. I'm not sure you were telling the truth. Sometimes I think you don't tell me everything because I worry too much. Maybe you think I react too much—not that I overreact, per se, but that I don't have to fight every battle. That it's okay to let some things go, not for the sake of the person or persons committing the injustices, but for our own energy, both physical and mental.

Once, when you were being discharged from the hospital, I mentioned I was going to bring some cookies for the nursing staff for being so good to you. You shook your head. "They weren't good to you?" I asked, slightly panicked and also ashamed I hadn't noticed. No, you said, not all of them. "Why didn't you tell me?" You looked up as if wishing for a higher power to knock sense into me. You'd been in the hospital for weeks and I'd been there every day, talking to doctors, asking questions, telling them your symptoms and asking what's next. You didn't want to add one more thing for me to contend with. You could deal with it. It wasn't that bad.

It's 2019 and Ellen, a staff person we really liked, called me. She never calls with good news and so I stood, paced around the kitchen, opened and closed cabinets. She told me everything was okay, but that she quit and she wanted me to know why.

"Okay," I said, although I was 100 percent sure it wasn't okay. Ellen was good at her job and unlike most of the staff, she seemed to really like it. Even better, she seemed especially to really like and understand Marcel.

She told me all in a rush how she noticed once that Marcel's call bell was unplugged and she thought it might be a mistake but then she said something about it to Marissa, and Marissa kind of laughed it off but then admitted he's a bit of a pain so, yes, they'd unplugged his call bell. Ellen told me Marissa told her the staff had been instructed to check on Marcel more often, but letting him have access to the call bell was driving everyone nuts. Marissa's words, not Ellen's.

I managed to ask Ellen if she thought Marcel was unreasonably ringing his call bell.

"No way," she said. She sounded close to tears.

"Okay," I said again. Still not okay. I started to wash my kitchen floor with a paper towel.

The next time I saw Marcel, I asked if he thought staff had been unplugging his call bell. He said yes, they have.

Marcel is smart and aware, and entirely unable to plug his call bell back in. He is unable to yell at anyone both because his voice box doesn't allow for yelling and also because he worries that any noise he makes will be too much noise and will make his staff more unhappy with him. He knows full well that when staff unplug his call bell, he will not be able to ask anyone to get him a drink of water or take him to the bathroom or put a movie into his DVD player. He won't be able to ask them to open the door of his room, open a window, get him a tissue. He won't be able to let anyone know if he doesn't feel well, if he's hot or cold or uncomfortable. He's stuck.

Ellen already reported this to the state agency that regulates group homes. I went ahead, with Marcel's permission, and reported it to Adult Protective Services and the State's ombudsman.

The next time we had Marcel's monthly meeting, I brought it up. Marissa denied it, but Marcel had already started to cry and I asked him if it was true and he said yes, it was.

"How do you know it's true?" Marissa asked. "It rings out in the hallway."

I had a hard time believing her argument was that Marcel wouldn't know if his call bell was plugged in or not because he might not hear it ring, but she didn't say anything else, so I said, "He knows it's true because he's seen them unplug it."

Marissa, still entirely straight-faced, said, "They must have been kidding around."

Marcel let out a wail of frustration. His case manager calmly asked for a resolution, for an agreement that the call bell will never be unplugged.

Marissa said of course it won't be unplugged, how can we ever think such a thing? This, I thought, is what it feels like to be gaslit.

After that meeting, I asked and Marcel reported that his call bell stayed plugged in. It's a small victory.

(Im)personal Care

The abuse of people with developmental disabilities has a long and horrific history, which extends from prehistoric to current times. Only in the past 20 or 30 years has society recognized that this abuse is a serious social problem and, with this recognition, research has been carried out on the topic. The limited research that has been done suggests differing causes for making this population so vulnerable to abuse. What is not under dispute is the fact that this abuse continues to this day, both in institutionalized care settings and in family care settings.

—C. Thornberry and K. Olson, *The Abuse of Individuals with Developmental Disabilities*

It was the Fourth of July in 2018 and I was on my back porch, which is an hour and a half away from Marcel, when a paramedic called. He wanted to know if they should take him to the hospital because his housemate hit him on the head "three or four times."

"Is he conscious?" I asked. I was shaking so hard I had to get off the chair I was sitting on and sit on the porch itself so that I didn't fall.

"Yes," the paramedic said.

"What did he hit him with?" In the weeks leading up to this, his housemate threw a chair and that was what I was picturing.

"His hands," the paramedic said. "His fists."

In the background, I heard Marcel make a noise. It was something between a wail and a moan. It's the noise he makes when he's upset and, to be honest, I was relieved to hear him make it because it meant he was lucid.

"Does he have a concussion?" I asked the paramedic who sounded young and had probably never encountered anyone like Marcel, someone who has a body that doesn't work very well but a mind that works just fine.

"No," the paramedic said. He hesitated. "But it might be safer for him to go to the hospital."

I could tell by the tone of his voice that he meant he couldn't guarantee Marcel wouldn't be hit again when he left. That he might be hurt worse the next time. I wanted to throw up.

"Does he want to go to the hospital?" I asked. *Say yes say yes say yes.* If I could get him in my car, I would drive up there and take him home with me even though we aren't set up to take care of him. We don't have a ramp so he could get in and out of the house, or a lift so he could get in and out of bed or on and off the toilet. We could get a ramp and a lift—we just need time. But every time I've offered, he's said he doesn't want me to take care of him, that he wants our friendship to be a space free from the kinds of hands-on care he gets from everyone else in his life. I say I understand this, even though there's a part of me that thinks he's wrong. Isn't safety more important than privacy?

The paramedic paused. Then he confessed he didn't know what Marcel wanted because he hadn't asked him. "Ask him," I said. *Please please please say you'll go to the hospital. I'll know you're safe in the hospital.*

The paramedic's voice shifted away from the phone. "Do you want to go to the hospital?"

Marcel grunted "No."

"No," the paramedic said. He sounded sincerely worried.

I closed my eyes. "You should probably do what he says unless you think he has a head injury and can't make good decisions." What I wanted to tell the paramedic was to take Marcel anyway, take him against his will, take him because the paramedic and I both knew what was best. Even though doing that would have gone against everything I've ever fought for on his behalf.

He paused. "He seems to know what he wants."

I told the paramedic to tell Marcel *I love you* and, while I was still on the other end of the phone, he did.

Later, Marcel tells me he was scared. This man, his housemate, gets suddenly, inexplicably angry and when that happens, he reminds Marcel of how volatile his brother could be. This time, the housemate was upset because the house staff told him he'd reached his daily quota of Pepsi.

After the hitting incident, the house staff will start locking Marcel in his room to keep his housemate from attacking him. This is the solution they come up with when I demand to know what they're going to do. This is the solution they tell Adult Protective Services when I file a complaint. Adult Protective Services agrees it's not ideal, but at least it's something. I am not appeased. Marcel seems resigned.

When we visit Marcel, we lock ourselves in his room and watch movies or play Wheel of Fortune on the Wii. Sometimes we hear the housemate screaming at house staff. Sometimes we lock Marcel in the room and go see if everything is okay, and when we see that no one is in immediate or critical danger, we ask staff to unlock his door and let us back in his room.

When I call the regional manager of the group home and demand to know why they placed a person with violent tendencies in a house with a person who cannot raise his hands or scream or even move his wheelchair away quickly, he acknowledges they made "an error in judgment." Policy, he tells me, will not allow the group home to move this individual until they find "appropriate placement" for him. I'm not heartless—I understand that this man is also disabled, just in a different way. Still, the situation is dangerous.

Marcel's options are to stay locked in his room unless the housemate is out of the house or go to a nursing home for respite care. If he chooses the nursing home, the group home could refuse to take him back. Instead of encouraging him to do what will make him feel safe, instead of reassuring him that he'll have housing to return to when it's safe for him to do so, the group home management has indicated that if he leaves, he will likely not be able to return.

Twenty years prior to the Fourth of July incident, when you lived in a nursing home and I was enrolled in a graduate program for documentary field studies, you agreed to be my subject.

One day, we talked about how you came to live in the nursing home. You'd been living in an apartment in Portland and had home health aides come in several times a day to get you up and dressed, help you get on and off the toilet, make and feed you food. You say it was hard to manage staff. I ask what you mean. You do that thing with your head like you don't know how to say it. I wait, but then I get tired of waiting. I ask if something specific happened.

I can't remember if you hesitated here. We were in the nursing home's small conference room, which used to be a physical therapy room with a hot tub and which, at this point in our friendship and for years afterword, still smelled like chlorine. It was also very hot in this room. We sat side by side, my straight-backed chair and your wheelchair turned slightly to face each other. My elbow kept banging the table. You sat slightly above elbow-banging height. I'm not sure if you said again only that something happened. If I pressed you. If it was clear you didn't want to tell me. Maybe you didn't want to tell me because you knew I'd get upset, or maybe you didn't want to tell me because you'd get upset.

I assumed you came to live in the nursing home because you're disabled and had no other options. Your parents were dead. I didn't yet know that your brother was also dead.

"Bed sores," you told me.

"Bed sores," I repeated. My grandmother was in a nursing home for eight years, so I know that bed sores can turn septic and deadly. I also know you get bed sores by being in one spot for too long, meaning no one has turned you, repositioned you, or possibly even checked on you. It made sense to me that you'd need to be somewhere they could monitor bed sores.

Yours got bad enough that you went into the hospital and then into a skilled rehab facility. And then you decided to move to the nursing home because it was "safer."

"Safer?" I thought you misspoke, that you meant easier. That having nursing staff or a doctor in the facility would be easier than going to an office to be treated.

Slowly, you typed into your communication device that "she" put you in the shower and went to Brunswick. Your communication device is a series of icons in which saved words and phrases are stored. "Brunswick" isn't in there, so you had to type it, but you can only spell phonetically, and Brunswick was a guessing game for you and a game of Clue for me. We got there, finally, but it took a lot out of us and we would probably have both preferred not to continue with this conversation. We could have talked about your upcoming plans to go to a Portland Pirates hockey game with your friend Connie and her family. Or, we could have talked about when you wanted help setting up your Christmas tree. Or if you'd had any more thoughts on what you wanted to buy the nursing staff this year. Last year, it was small tins of butter cookies, one for every person who takes care of you. I wrote more than twenty names on Christmas tags and affixed them under red and green bows on the little tins.

But my curiosity and outrage wouldn't let it go. "Why safer? What happened?" I asked. It's at least thirty minutes one way from Portland to Brunswick and that's not counting traffic. I stopped myself from asking how this could happen because it would sound like I was blaming you and I know you well enough to know you already blamed yourself. For having to be cared for. For having cerebral palsy. This seemed crazy—that a person who is disabled, who was born disabled, could blame himself for the condition, or at least the burden of the condition. And yet, you told me that the Catholic faith in which you were raised led you and your parents to believe your disability was a manifestation of sin. Theirs, probably, but possibly they meant the sin you were both with, the sin Catholics believe we are all born with. "Original sin," which sounds like something creative but isn't.

"The health worker," you typed into your communication device.

"The person taking care of you," I said, just to make sure I was getting this right, "Put you in the shower and left?"

You nodded

"With the water running?" I asked.

You looked at me like I'd just asked a really dumb question, but my mind was trying to make it so you were fully clothed, dry, and just hanging out in your bathroom for an hour or more. Just like you'd hang out in your living room or bedroom. Maybe there was even some country music playing. In my version of events, you were not wet and naked and very, very afraid.

"Yes," you said.

"How long was she gone?" I asked.

You didn't know. A while. A long time.

"But," I sputtered. "Why?" As if there was a good reason. As if a good reason would make it better. There must have been an emergency. Maybe she put you in there and looked at the time and realized she was late to pick up her kid at daycare and maybe this had been the third or fourth time and they'd warned her this would be the last time. Maybe if she was late picking up the kid, she'd lose her daycare and then she'd lose her job and maybe it was her mother who used to pick up the kid but her mother died two months ago. Maybe she really thought she could be quick—twenty minutes, tops. Maybe she'd always been a terrible judge of time. Maybe she hadn't figured on the water going cold or you being scared. Maybe it took longer than she expected because there was traffic or traffic was slow and no matter what else she definitely couldn't speed, couldn't get stopped and try to explain to the cop she'd left a disabled guy in the shower. And then when she finally got back and you asked her if she was all right—because you were worried something had happened to her—maybe she felt terrible.

"The water went cold?" I asked.

"Yes," you said. But, worse than that, you thought you might drown. If your shower chair tipped and you'd landed with your face up, you may not have been able to close your mouth. Or, if you landed face down, you might have been face down in a puddle. You can't initiate a roll to either side. You can't sit up. You can't stand.

If you'd fallen, you might have hit your head.

Or you could have gotten hypothermia.

But none of that happened. She came back after an hour or two and got you out of the shower. She didn't offer an explanation. Maybe she thought you hadn't noticed how long she was gone.

"Did you fire her?" I asked. There I go, blaming the victim.

You looked at me, then finally grunted "no." You tell me that if you fired her, there would have been no one to come the next day.

"You could have just hired someone else," I said. Which was a ridiculous thing to say. I didn't realize it yet, because at this point in our friendship I hadn't seen much of it, but it's very hard to find people who are good at taking care of other people, especially when the only person holding them accountable is the person they are supposed to be taking care of.

I almost said this shower-leaving woman could still be out there, could still be behaving negligently in other situations. How could you let her get away with that? I stopped myself only because your eyes filled with tears.

On a different day, we talked about what it would have taken to fire that woman. You would have had to ask someone who worked for you, someone who likely worked for the same agency this woman worked for and probably knew her, to call the agency and report what happened to you. You would have had to trust both the person you asked to call and the person who took the information at the agency to believe you and follow through with firing this woman. If they didn't fire her but disciplined her or simply told her about your complaint, she could do something much worse than leave you in the shower. Plus, you still needed someone to get you out of bed. There was always the actual possibility that there would not be enough staff and that no one would come.

I didn't want to keep talking about this because I hated things I couldn't fix. I've learned, over the years, to leave more space for you to tell me hard things. It's a thing I love when my friends do for me. It's something you always do for me.

You told me it was just that one time she left you in the shower. I had, I think, made you feel guilty for not trying hard enough.

She wasn't the only bad experience you had, although she was the worst.

Over time, I learned about the woman who brought her kid and let the kid color your coffee table with crayons. She probably meant for the kid to use the crayons on a coloring book on the coffee table, but the kid used them on the table, as kids do, and the woman just left the crayon marks, the table ruined.

"She didn't clean it or offer to get you a new table?" I asked.

You shook your head.

And then there was the guy who stole your credit cards and ran up a big bill. Your aunt Leta told us the story in a way that slanted toward how much your Uncle Gil ended up paying the credit card company. Maybe this was so long ago things were different, but I wondered why the credit card company made you pay. I've had credit cards stolen and I didn't end up paying any of the thousands of dollars racked up by the thief. Your aunt couldn't say. It was a long time after that before you got a debit card.

You ended up with bed sores because help didn't show up when they were supposed to and you stayed in one position for too long. Pressure-point sores show up and then, if they aren't monitored, they can open up and get infected. The bed sores went septic, meaning you had infection running through your body and had to be put on heavy-duty antibiotics in the hospital. For someone like you who is already compromised because you have an overarching disease, infection can be a death sentence.

You had a button that you could use to call for help. The button was mounted next to your bed and, once, after you'd been in bed for several days, you hit it.

You thought you'd hit the button and maybe someone would have a key and let themselves in. You did not expect the fire department to break down the door. You did not expect men in full fire gear to burst into your room. You tell me you were terrified. I deflect, as I sometimes do, and make a joke that if they'd given you a heart attack, at least they could have revived you. You laugh along with me, even though we're both crying a little.

After that, you never hit the button again.

The bed sores eventually healed, but you decided to stay in the nursing home. I think it was your friend Becki who once told me you traded freedom for security. You gave up your own apartment for a single bedroom shared with a roommate, a bathroom shared by four people. You gave up the ability to keep most of your money, because nursing homes keep most of your Medicare and Medicaid. Because having an institution in charge of your care, where there are lots of people to make sure you get in and out of bed, seemed more manageable than trusting people to do the job they were paid to do.

Nearly two decades after moving into the nursing home, Marcel moved into a group home. In part he made this leap because I promised to always advocate for him once he was there. I swore I would never let anything bad happen to him. This is a promise it turns out I can't keep, not entirely.

The first time I offered to move him out of the group home and have him come live with us, I hadn't even talked to Steve about it. All three of us were in a meeting with his case worker, Big M, and the regional director. He started to cry because the house manager said "You know I'd never let anything happen to you" in a tone that was like a mess of melted candy.

To Big M, I said, "You're a bully and a liar." Steve squeezed my knee under the table. He wasn't trying to shut me up, he just didn't want me to punch her. I've never punched anyone, but I might have punched her.

Later, she'd be fired and we'd find out she had been ordering medical supplies with residents' Medicare and Medicaid funding—a hospital bed, among other things—and then selling the items and pocketing the money. All I knew in this meeting was that she hadn't submitted the paperwork for Marcel to get a shower chair. She hadn't made the call to get Marcel into a psychologist to help deal with the depression he'd been feeling. She'd "forgotten" to tell staff about plans I confirmed with her to bring Marcel to a diner for lunch, an afternoon of bowling, and an evening to look at Christmas lights. She said they're short-staffed, which was the same excuse I heard no less than thirty times in the year he'd been in this home.

"I promise we're working on it," the regional director said.

She's said this before. That's when he started crying and I said, "You can live with us."

"Is that something you'd want, Marcel?" his case manager asked.

He typed, "I don't know" into his communication device.

On the car ride home, Steve asked how Marcel living with us would work, in a practical sense. I talked about converting the den into a bedroom and putting a roll-in shower in the downstairs bathroom, which would mean bumping out the house or losing part of the kitchen or living room. I talked about ramps being installed. "Or we could just move," I said. To Steve's great credit, he did not say no. He was as shaken as I was by how terrible things had been since Marcel moved to the group home and by how little it seemed we could do.

The next time we saw Marcel, I brought it up again. He said no, he doesn't want to come live with us.

I said, "I know you worry about privacy, but we'll hire people to do your personal care."

He looked at me.

"And what if they don't show up?" Steve said.

Marcel looked at Steve, grateful, and nodded.

I clenched my teeth. "We can call the next person on the list. We'll only help you with personal stuff as a last resort."

Still, Marcel shook his head. He knew how these things went. He knew we'd have to do personal care and that, once that line was crossed, it can't be uncrossed. We also all acknowledged that liking someone and wanting to live with someone are two different things. And that, if he hated living with us, how would he tell us? How would we help him advocate if it's us he needed to advocate against?

We talked about this off and on for a few months, until the house manager was fired and Marcel got another one and another one and another one and another one. The last one was almost as bad as the first and she's the one under whose supervision the hitting happened. Still, Marcel doesn't want to live with us.

Maybe all he needed to know was that we'd take him in if he wanted us to. Small comfort, but it's something.

Your Call Is Important to Us

The transportation provisions of Title II cover public transportation services, such as city buses and public rail transit (e.g., subways, commuter rails, Amtrak). Public transportation authorities may not discriminate against people with disabilities in the provision of their services.

—Americans with Disabilities Act

It's 2021 and Marcel wanted to ride the train. He'd never been on a train and he saw them all the time, especially from his hospital rooms in Portland during his frequent stays. It's during one of his stays that I promised we'd ride the train. It was, more or less, meant to give him something to look forward to. During other hospital stays, I'd registered him for summer camp, bought us tickets to concerts, and bought him new sneakers.

There was no way to get handicapped-accessible train tickets online—the little handicapped symbol was grayed out when I tried to click on it, even when I tried different dates and times. So I called, and an automated operator told me it would be a thirty-minute wait.

I'd already scoured the Amtrak website, but I did it again while I waited. Thirty minutes isn't too bad. I re-read everything they have to say about their handicapped accessibility. One thing: They offered a discount if you provided proof of your disability. It made me laugh to think that Marcel, who can't stand or use his arms or talk, would need to be a card-carrying disabled person in order to receive a discount. That looking at him wouldn't be enough. They'll take a letter from a physician or a "membership card from a disability organization." I had no idea what the latter was—what organization? How do you get a membership? The next time I saw Marcel. I told him about my wait on hold and the "membership card" and he had no idea what it was, either.

What was especially problematic about the Amtrak offer was that the disabled person wouldn't be able to get the discount unless he or she showed up in person to provide proof of the disability. That meant that a person couldn't have a friend or staff person or family member call and book them a ticket and still get the discount. I guess you're supposed to just show up (somehow), show your letter or disability card, and hope there are accessible seats available. I get that this is to prevent people from fraudulently purchasing handicapped tickets, which I've heard happens (for the extra leg room), but it seems like the people being punished here are the disabled people.

Years later, I scoured the Amtrak website looking for this card-carrying caveat, but it's gone. It's possible I'm misremembering it, but it's more likely someone at Amtrak realized they were setting an impossible task.

There was a tinny instrumental of "Bridge Over Troubled Waters" playing. It was pretty terrible, but I was already ten minutes into my thirty-minute wait.

While I was on hold, I went as far as starting to book two round-trip tickets online for the next day from Portland to Brunswick. I thought maybe they'd offer me a handicapped option before I checkout. They didn't so I left the page without completing the order.

By now, it had already been close to thirty minutes so someone would be helping me shortly. They're answering the calls in the order they're received. My call is important to them.

For hockey games at our local arena, we can't buy handicapped tickets online or via phone. We have to drive an hour to go to the box office to purchase them in person because, as we've been told repeatedly, the computer system doesn't allow for the phone agent to select specific seats. To get seats that are not up or down a flight of stairs, we have to select them with an in-person ticket agent. When we've complained about the inaccessibility of this, the downright *not*-accessibility of it, we've been assured that if we purchased a ticket in a non-handicapped spot, arena staff would move Marcel to a handicapped spot. They wouldn't necessarily move Steve and me so we could sit near him, though, because handicapped seating is really limited. The only way for us to sit with Marcel in handicapped seating is to buy three tickets together. Which has to be done in person at the box office.

We've been told, when we complain that this means we drive an hour each way just to buy tickets, that we can always buy them the day of the game. But if we wait until the day of the game, Marcel often can't maneuver through the throng of people already in line to get tickets or get to their seats. Also, the handicapped seating could very well be sold out by then because there are only two handicapped sections with five or six removable seats in them. So, when we want to go to a hockey game, Steve makes a separate trip on a separate day to ensure Marcel gets a handicapped seat and we get to sit next to him. We've just gotten used to it by now.

After forty minutes on hold with Amtrak, I started cooking tomorrow night's macaroni and cheese dinner. I boiled pasta, made a roux, grated cheese and half an onion. "Bridge Over Troubled Waters" came on four more times. My call was still important to them.

The train ride itself will take about a half hour, then we'll have a little more than two hours in Brunswick, then the half-hour ride back to Portland. The choices on the website were for child, adult, or senior tickets. The information under the handicapped accessibility tab said there was special seating available if the person couldn't transfer out of their wheelchair, which is the case for Marcel. Nowhere did it say how to obtain such tickets. I considered sending an email. But surely someone would answer my call shortly and that would be easier with follow-up questions. I needed to ask about a lip or gap between the platform and the train and, if there was one, make sure they had some kind of ramp. I needed to ask if COVID restrictions were still in place and, if so, a face shield rather than a mask would suffice because Marcel can't keep a face mask in place—his lower jaw muscles shift too much.

It'd been an hour. If I hung up now, no one would blame me. No one would say I didn't try to get tickets.

I was nervous about this trip, because we hadn't done a train ride before. I was worried about how handicapped accessible the platform is. I called Amtrak a year ago, pre-pandemic, and spoke to a pleasant woman who seemed knowledgeable and assured me everything was very very handicapped accessible. But we've been told a place is handicapped accessible only to find a two-inch lip over the door frame. Which isn't much if you're in a manual wheelchair that can be tipped back and bumped over obstacles. But Marcel isn't in that kind of wheelchair. His chair weighs about two hundred pounds and is more like a mobility scooter.

We've been told theaters are handicapped accessible only to find a step or steps, too-narrow doorways, or not enough seating space for his chair. Once, at a concert, we moved the folding chair next to the folding chair that was taken out for Marcel's chair only to be scolded, told next time we'd have to buy two seats. His chair isn't that big; it's just bigger than what most spaces can accommodate.

Normally, I'd just go check out the train myself. But I don't think I can actually look at the train without buying a ticket, and I don't want to buy one just for myself and then potentially hold up a line of people while I inspect the platform. I was just going to have to take the ticket agent's word for it. If I ever got to talk to a ticket agent.

After an hour and ten minutes, I plugged in my phone to charge.

I was worried about how hard or easy it would be to get Marcel on and off the train and how much space he'd have to turn his chair once he was on the train. I was worried about how quickly the doors would close or if they would stay open long enough not to threaten to squeeze him or catch the bag he keeps on the back of his chair and drag him over. Automatic doors, elevator doors, sidewalk signals, and all kinds of helpful amenities never allocate enough time for Marcel's level of disability.

At an hour and fifteen minutes, I unplugged my phone, careful not to disconnect the call, and took the dog out. If I disconnected, I'd have to call back. I didn't want to give up on something reasonably easy when Marcel's whole life is so hard.

It wasn't that I didn't want to go on the train ride with him. I love the pleasure on Marcel's face when he's having a good time. I love making him laugh. But I was worried that he hadn't been feeling well. He hates not feeling well and so he often denies he isn't feeling well. I was worried the ride-time combined with the stopping-time would be too much time, even though Marcel will say it'll be fine. I used to trust him to know his limits, but lately I've seen him slump over from too much sun or after a long day or after he's eaten something hard to digest. I worried because he, like everyone, forgets or denies the limits of his aging body.

But still, I waited on hold. I was back inside with the dog, phone plugged in again. I drained the pasta, mixed it into the cheese sauce, and layered it into two ramekins.

I worried Marcel would need his ileostomy bag burped while we were out. He doesn't like me to burp the bag for him because he doesn't want to subject me to what is undeniably a gross task. Steve won't be able to go on the train ride with us. Marcel doesn't mind him burping the bag, maybe because he's a man and he has all the same body parts. Maybe because ours is the only relationship Marcel has that doesn't involve some kind of personal care. Feeding him doesn't count because eating together is social. Letting the air out of a bag full of poop is not social. I worried Marcel won't tell me when the bag needs to be burped and that I won't notice and that it will leak or explode. This can, in theory, cause skin breakdown, but it's also just plain embarrassing. There's nothing wrong with his sense of smell.

An hour and a half into my eternal hold, I got a call from work. Even though I almost never got phone calls from work and even though someone might really need something, I didn't answer it because I was afraid I'd disconnect Amtrak.

I could have written a letter to Amtrak while I was on hold. I could have asked them why they didn't make this process easier. I could have pointed out how impossible it would be for someone like Marcel to get handicapped tickets without the help of someone else, which is the opposite of independence, which is presumably what train travel is all about. I once wrote a letter to the City of Auburn about a pothole twice the width of Marcel's chair, a hole that necessitated that he turn around and go back to the nursing home where there was a curb cut and a crosswalk, and we basically had to start the walk to Dairy Queen all over again. Much to our astonishment, they fixed the hole right away.

One hour and forty minutes in, I got a text from work and this time I looked at it. The text was just to say everything was fine, disregard the phone call. At this point, I was starting to think I might be on hold for the rest of my life.

At one hour and fifty minutes, I unplugged my phone and took the dog out again. She barked at a squirrel. Now was when someone would answer, I thought, when I couldn't hear, when I was calling the dog to come, when she was ignoring me and I was walking across the lawn in my bare feet and I stepped on a rock and swore. But, no, no one answered.

I had had a nightmare about Marcel the other night. I have a lot of nightmares but almost none about him, at least not directly. In this one, he's on the beach. I'm nearby, but somewhere behind him. A crane comes down and attaches to his chair like that claw game where the claw picks up stuffed animals and other small toys and deposits them into a chute. The claw lifts him up. I watch, immobile, murmuring *no no no no no no*. He's in the air. He looks terrified. I can't do anything. The claw drops him and his face contorts and I wake up yelling, Steve and the dog staring at me.

I was still on hold. I came inside with the dog, who finally gave up on the squirrel. I plugged in the phone and wiped down the counter. I was across the room when I heard someone ask how he could help me. I ignored it as part of the music at first, but then I dashed across the room, shouting, "A person! A real person!" He laughed like I might be crazy. "I'm sorry," I said. "I've been on hold for two hours and six minutes." Nonplussed, he asked how he could help me. He was pleasant enough, but he didn't apologize. I suppose it wasn't his fault. It wasn't like he'd been on break the whole time. He'd probably been trained not to apologize, which would open a door to criticism. He'd probably been on the phone all day and it isn't his fault the handicapped selection on the website was grayed out.

I explained what I was looking for and when. I told him the handicapped tickets on the website were grayed out, but he didn't acknowledge he heard me. He asked me to hold. I groaned. I can't hold. I absolutely can't hold. If he put me on hold, it would be the third circle of hell. I huffed a hysterical laugh, but he didn't seem to catch on to my unraveling. He put me on hold. This time there was silence and I was sure he hung up on me and I walked in circles around my kitchen. A few seconds later, he came back on the line and confirmed the tickets for the next day. I was so relieved I nearly started to cry. "Anything else?" he asked.

I told him I saw that Amtrak was still requiring face masks but I assumed a face shield was okay for Marcel, seeing the Centers for Disease Control didn't recommend tight-fitting masks for people who can't remove them on their own. He hesitated. "I'm sorry," he said. "It has to be a tight-fitting mask over the mouth and nose."

I didn't explain Marcel's face to him, the way it moved of its own accord, often dislodging a paper mask. I didn't explain his arms, which could never reach up and remove a mask if he couldn't breathe. I should have asked to speak to a manager. But I didn't. I said well, that won't work. I said I'd call back in the fall.

I was relieved we wouldn't have to try out this train trip. I was ashamed of my relief.

Maybe I'm not as brave as I was when I was twenty-one, when we first met and I operated under the belief that anything was possible. Maybe I'm not as reckless and maybe that's because I'm getting older or maybe it's because you don't bounce back as fast as you used to. Maybe I've come to rely on Steve's steadying presence alongside me when we take you places and, because he couldn't come on this train ride, I didn't really want to go. Maybe I'm just not as good at trying new things as I was twenty-five years ago. Maybe I'm rightfully anxious, because you've been sick more and more and I desperately want to fulfill your wishes, but nervous you'll be sick on the train. Or that you'll get COVID and it'll be much worse than the first or second time you had it. And that will be my fault, even though I advocate over and over for your autonomy. Even though I know you know the risks. Still, I feel responsible for you. Or, if not responsible, then protective.

We agreed to meet for a walk instead of the train ride, and I assured Marcel I'd call Amtrak in the fall and we'd try again. He wasn't upset. He felt bad I had to wait on hold for so long and it turned out to be a waste of time. But he was also frustrated it's this hard to buy handicapped tickets.

He told me I should write this essay.

A year later, Marcel asked about a train ride again. The worst of COVID was over, and so I checked the Amtrak website and saw they were no longer requiring masks. Also, mysteriously, miraculously, I could click on the little wheelchair and purchase handicapped tickets. It was no longer grayed out. I bought the tickets, forgetting most of my anxiety about the lip on the platform, the adequate open time of the doors, the amount of space for Marcel to park his chair.

We got to the train station in plenty of time. The train was late, but we didn't care. We like to people-watch. It was hot in the covered greenhouse-like tube we waited in, and several people approached me to say there's air conditioning in the building, that I should take Marcel inside. They came right out and said this, in front of him, and I knew they meant well, but the underlying assumption was that he can't determine what he wants and/or I hadn't bothered to ask. I tried to be polite, because Marcel is unfailingly polite. I laughed and told everyone that he loves the heat, that I was the one who was sweating to death. Marcel looked at me and cocked his head. He was asking if I wanted to go inside. "No," I said. "I'm just being melodramatic."

Getting on the train was a little tricky. The doorway was narrow and there was just barely enough room for Marcel to get in and turn into the narrow passageway that then opened up into the spacious seating area. Once he was in, we were golden. There was no one else in this section and so we sat and looked out the windows. From time to time, I recognized a building from the back and I pointed it out to him: the hospital, the place that used to be a Chinese restaurant that is now a sun tanning place, the Rite Aid that's now closed.

We arrived in Brunswick, and when he got to the doorway I realized we had a problem. I was behind him as he went to make the turn to get onto the platform, except he couldn't make the turn. His chair was too long. What I mean is he could have made the turn if we took off the footrest and, well, cut off his feet. I was stuck behind him, with no room at all on either side of the chair so I could assess the situation from that side or go get help. I tried to give the chair a push, but all it did was wedge Marcel's feet into the door jamb. I was sweating, but I leaned over and told him we'd figure this out, because of course we would. We had to. He couldn't be stuck on an Amtrak train for the rest of his life. And then like magic, Steve was there. He showed up to surprise us, not to rescue us, but that's what he and the conductor did as they rocked Marcel's chair inches at a time to turn him enough so he could exit the train.

In Brunswick, we ate ice cream and walked around and I tried not to think about how we were going to get off the train when we got to Portland and Steve wasn't there. I'd make sure there was no tilt to the chair when we exited. That should give us the extra inches he needed to turn. Maybe I'd put the chair in manual. Or maybe Marcel would let me drive it, just for those few seconds. I tried to ignore the anxiety in my stomach. I mean, there had to be a way to get him off the train, right? There wasn't much we can do about it now—we're here and we had to get back.

When it was time to leave, Marcel got back on the train without a problem. I tried to enjoy the ride back. We didn't talk about what we were going to do until we were just about to pull into the station. I told him my thoughts about putting the chair as upright as it would go and he agreed. When he's upright, I slid his feet back on the footrests as far as I could. We both held our breath.

He got stuck anyway. He inched back and turned, over and over, but he couldn't gain the inches he needed. I tried to rock the chair but it was way too heavy for me to do it on my own and no one came to offer help. Everyone exited the train via doors we weren't blocking. Marcel's staff person texted me and then texted me again and again to say she heard the train pull in, she sees all the people, where were we? I texted back that we're stuck. We'll be out as soon as possible. She didn't text me back a surprised face or anything. Just a thumbs up.

Finally, a conductor came by. "Are you stuck?" he asked.

Obviously, I thought. But I smiled and said yes. I was trying to not be flustered because I didn't want Marcel to be embarrassed. The conductor was very nice. He said Amtrak was planning to make their doorways bigger in the next five years. He laughed and said that doesn't help us at the moment. Together, he and I rocked the chair. Marcel bounced and jostled and I could see from his face this was both frightening and uncomfortable for him, but there was nothing I could do to make this better. I was mad at myself for not checking out the train before we rode, but I don't honestly know if I would have noticed the short turning radius he'd need to exit.

It took almost a half hour to finally free Marcel from the train. I sweated through my shirt, and my arms were shaking from lifting and pushing his chair. My legs and back ached. Marcel was looking down, frowning. I could tell he was embarrassed, that he felt bad we held up the train, and that he needed so much help.

"Hey," I said, putting my arm around him as we walked and rolled away from the departing train. "This isn't your fault, you know. It's a bad design."

He nodded, but he's still frowning.

I punched his shoulder. "It was an adventure," I said. And then, a few steps later, "But let's not do it again." That finally got him to laugh and I laughed, too.

When You Die

Surprisingly little is known at the population level about the ripple effects of child disability on the family. Studies in the psychology literature indicate that a number of specific child health conditions are associated with poor mental health outcomes of parents and siblings, but empirical research on the impacts of child disability on resources, hardship, and physical health of family members is scant.

—Impact of Child Disability on the Family,
Nancy E Reichman, Hope Corman, Kelly Noonan

Let's assume you die before I do. You're twenty-five years older than I am and you have cerebral palsy, which isn't a death sentence but which definitely puts you at a disadvantage, longevity-wise.

I've been in the room with you while a priest gives you Last Rites—twice. I've stood by your side while you refused to sign a DNR on more than one occasion. But I can only remember discussing the practicalities of death once. "You have a pre-paid funeral," your case manager said during a meeting in which we were going over your care plan. You nodded. This was news to me, but I was proud of you for your forethought and a little relieved that I wouldn't have to pick out your casket or the music played at the funeral. At least, I assume that's part of what gets paid for with a pre-paid funeral. We were both raised Catholic and the Catholic traditions around death can be elaborate, expensive, and particular.

Then your case manager said, "Your cousin Nancy has the plans."

You nodded.

I tried to mentally catalog the handful of relatives I've met. I'm almost certain I've never met Nancy. "Nancy?" I ask. "Is she local?"

You nod.

"And we have her phone number?" What I want to ask if we even know if she's still alive, but I can't think of a delicate way to say this.

"Yes," you say.

"Have you heard from her in. . . a while?" Maybe we've run into her at one of the wakes we've attended.

"No," you say.

Your case manager moves on so I assume I have nothing to worry about. Maybe someone being in charge of your pre-paid funeral is no big deal. Maybe Nancy will get in touch when the time comes. A person can't forget they're in charge of another person's funeral arrangements, can they? Even if they haven't seen that person in decades? Maybe I'm discomforted for no good reason.

I do not spend all my time worrying about what will happen when Marcel dies. But I do think about it, because I know it will be one of the hardest things I'll ever have to go through.

SCENARIO I

Someone from the group home will notify me of his death. I'll find Nancy through one of Marcel's cousins on Facebook, or maybe she'll find me. She'll ask for photographs for the wake and I'll print out some of the best ones, the ones from camp, from concerts, from restaurants. I'll feel good about giving her the photographs and it won't even cross my mind that she and other members of his family will say how much they miss him, even though they were right down the street from him for years and never visited. They'll say they're grateful he had us, and we'll smile and say we were grateful to have him.

I'll put on a black dress and closed-toe black shoes. Steve will wear a tie and jacket.

I'll sign the guest book at the wake. We will kneel and pray by Marcel's casket. When we stand, we will move through the receiving line and tell his cousins it's nice to meet them. We might feel a little resentment at all the times they didn't visit him, but it's too late now and Steve and I will be able to let go of our resentment and just feel sad to have lost Marcel. We'll be at peace with the knowledge that we did everything we could for him and that these cousins have missed out on knowing him.

At the funeral, I'll get up and tell a story—probably the one about the time I got him stuck on the beach. We both thought the sand at the end of the wooden walkway wasn't that deep, although I didn't go ahead of him and test it out like I usually do with unknown surfaces. The sand was four inches of powder. We looked at each other as soon as he rolled off the wooden pier and knew we were in trouble. Marcel moved his speed from turtle to rabbit, but it didn't matter because his wheels just spun and spun. As people moved around us—some looking at us, some deliberately not looking at us—I put Marcel's chair in manual mode and rocked it back and forth incrementally, just like I do when I get my car stuck in the snow (which happens more than I like to admit). It worked, finally, and Marcel was able to roll back onto the wooden slats. We both laughed then. "Let's just look at the beach from here," I said once we were back on the wooden pier. He laughed and raised his arm to tap me on the head.

I'll tell that story and Marcel's family will laugh, and I guess I have this fantasy they'll now wish they'd spent more time with him.

In this version of events, Steve and I go to the reception after the funeral. We eat cheese cubes and strawberries speared on toothpicks. We stay long enough to hear Marcel's family tell us how much it meant to them, over the years, to know we were in his life. What a comfort it was to them. How it lessened their own guilt. Steve and I will smile and be gracious and we'll go home feeling good about the way we handled things.

SCENARIO II

Someone from the group home will call to tell me Marcel has passed away. His cousin Nancy, or maybe one of his other cousins whom I've never met or met once decades ago, will send me a message on Facebook to let me know when the services are.

I'll tell Steve I don't want to go. I'll say we have so many memories with Marcel alive and I want to hold onto those, to preserve those. I'll say I don't want to see his family pretending to be sad, because of course their sadness could only be for show. How could they be sad when they haven't had anything to do with him in more than twenty-five years? They don't get to be sad. I can hear myself telling this to my therapist, and my therapist kindly and gently waiting for me to round the bend to the conclusion that everyone is entitled to grief, no matter the circumstances.

Steve will say we should go to the services. The wake at least. He'll say Marcel would want us to go. He'll remind me of the wakes we've taken him to because the saying goodbye ritual is important to him.

I'll agree to go to the wake, mostly because if there's an afterlife, I don't want to have to explain to Marcel why I didn't go.

I'll put on my black dress and closed-toed shoes and Steve will put on his tie and jacket.

At the wake, one of the cousins will thank us for being your "angels," which is a term they've used on Facebook every time we post pictures of Marcel and me or Marcel and Steve or Marcel and me and Steve and the dog. I will look this cousin in the eye and tell her to fuck off.

Steve will gentle me back to the car. I'll rant on the way home—about how no one came to visit Marcel while he was alive. About how they have no right to be sad. About how all of this is just posturing. Steve will listen. He'll tell me we never did anything for them, only for Marcel.

SCENARIO III

Someone from the group home will call to tell me Marcel has died. Nancy or one of the other cousins will send me a Facebook message to let me know when the services are. Despite Steve's very reasonable arguments, I'll refuse to go to the wake or funeral. I'll stand firm in my belief that I have all the memories of Marcel I want and need, that he would understand why I refuse to go, and that I don't want to be around his family and their pretend grief. I won't be swayed by the argument that they might have actual grief.

I'll stay home on the days of his wake and funeral. I'll stay in my pajamas. I'll watch the clock and know this is the time the priest is praying, Marcel's casket behind him. Now is the time of the funeral Mass. Now is the time he's being lowered into the ground.

I'll feel guilty. I'll eat cereal and cry. Steve will kindly not tell me he told me so.

Some months later, we'll go to the cemetery where Marcel's mother, father, and brother are buried. His placard has been in place as long as I've known him, engraved with his name and date of birth. Waiting, all these years, for the date of his death.

I'll bring flowers for all four graves. Lilacs if they're in season. Something orange otherwise. I'll say a prayer. Steve and I will tell each other stories—the time Marcel and Steve saw the pretty nurse before I did because I was too busy yammering on about shoes and they were ogling her. The time I beat both Marcel and Steve in archery at camp. The time Marcel made me feed him steamers at Old Orchard Beach and I complained the whole time because of how slimy they are. The time Marcel showed up for my graduation and surprised me. The time we surprised Marcel with a new TV.

Steve and I will laugh and cry. We won't stay at the grave long because Marcel isn't there, anyway. His body is there, but Marcel, the essential him, is in our memories.

SCENARIO IV

The group home will assume Nancy has told me Marcel died and Nancy won't have told me because she assumes the group home has told me. I'll send Marcel a text like I always do so we can plan the next weekend's activities and when I don't hear back in a day, two days, four days, I'll call the group home. Someone will stammer through an explanation. There will be apologies, but it won't matter by then because it will be too late. Steve and I will have missed the services.

Steve and I will go to the cemetery where Marcel's place marker has been engraved with his name and date of birth, a hyphen waiting for the end date. Maybe it won't be filled in when we go visit. Maybe Nancy will forget to have it done. Maybe we'll get to pretend that Marcel lives forever.

SCENARIO V

Someone from the group home will call to tell me Marcel died. They'll say they tried to get in touch with Nancy, but the number they have for her is no longer working. They'll say they tried the funeral parlor listed, but the funeral parlor says they have no record of his arrangements.

The person from the group home will ask what I want to do and I'll say I have to get back to them.

Marcel and I have never talked about the details he wants for a funeral.

I decide on a medium-priced casket with an orange silk interior, a bouquet of orange lilies for the top, a rosary for his hands. He has dress pants and a white shirt and a red-striped tie. I pick out pictures to be displayed at the wake, "Amazing Grace" to be sung at the funeral. I write his obituary. I will mention that he was the son of Emilienne and Leonard, that he was predeceased by them and his stepfather, Gerald, and his brother, George. I will say he lived a long and happy life, despite the challenges of cerebral palsy. I will say he loved hockey, eating out, music, and the beach. I will say he never lost his curiosity, never stopped wanting to learn new things, explore new places. I will ask that donations be made to Pine Tree Camp in lieu of flowers.

We will have the wake and funeral because that's what Marcel would have wanted. We will never hear from Nancy. We'll never know what happened to the pre-paid arrangements. We'll have our suspicions.

I hope there's an "after." I hope I get to see you again and that you are whatever version of yourself you want to be—whatever version makes you happiest and most comfortable. If that means full use of your arms, legs, and voice, that's great, I'd want that, too. But I'd also be happy to have you be the you you've always been. Just without the pain, the suffering, the marginalization. We'll sit on a cloud and eat chocolate-peanut butter ice cream and watch a hockey game while listening to Johnny Cash and Tammy Wynette.

There will be the in-between time, too. The time between when you die and when I die. I'm not sure of who I'll be without you.

You Say It's Your Birthday

> *The usual cerebral palsy life expectancy in non-ambulatory children with quadriplegic spastic cerebral palsy is around 40 years.*
>
> —Trishla Foundation

For his seventieth birthday, I planned on throwing Marcel a party with country music, balloons, and fireworks, all of it backdropped by a meal of steak, gravy, and mashed potatoes. I would have invited his friends and probably, because he would have wanted me to, his family.

But we can't have a party because there's a pandemic. We need to celebrate, though, because he's turning seventy and he has cerebral palsy and more than one medical professional has expressed astonishment that he's still alive.

And, so, when his beloved Pine Tree Camp opens up for day passes, we jump at the chance to go on his actual birthday. Usually, Marcel attends Pine Tree Camp for five days in the summer. He stays in a cabin with other people who have cerebral palsy or similar physical disabilities, and he's treated like the sentient person he is. Counselors ask what kind of privacy he likes when using the toilet. They ask what he likes to eat and how he likes to eat it. They take him swimming and boating. If he chooses to, he gets to spend one night of the week camping on the ground in a sleeping bag and tent instead of a bed in the cabin. There's a fully handicapped-accessible treehouse, a playground for the younger kids who come on different weeks, a barn with goats and chickens. There's archery, boating, kayaking, swimming, crafts, dancing, and biking—all adapted. There are wide, flat paths and acres and acres to explore.

Marcel's seventieth birthday is a bright and beautiful day in early October. He and his house staff and housemate, Stephanie, are waiting at a picnic table by the time Steve and I get there. There's a banner just above him: *Happy Birthday, Marcel!* I burst into tears. He rolls his eyes at me.

Pre-COVID, I imagined throwing him the party I was going to throw him for his sixtieth—when his cousin Amy insisted that she host—but better. That year, I'd rented a hall, hired a country music singer named Vicki Lee, planned to have chocolate cake with chocolate icing and hockey-themed decorations. But, Marcel's cousin, Amy, was working at the nursing home where he lived at the time and, when she caught wind of my plans, she decided she should be the one to throw the party.

I didn't argue with Amy because I wanted his family to be in his life. I wanted them to see him more often than at the two times we'd taken you to wakes and they came up, one by one, as if he were the deceased, and said how much they missed him. At one point, Steve asked one of Marcel's cousins if he knew that he lived in the nursing home just down the street.

"I know it," the cousin said. He was chagrinned, but he quickly recovered. "I keep meaning to stop. One of these nights on my way home from work, I'll come in for a visit." Marcel lit up with anticipation.

"You'd like that, buddy?" the cousin said.

"He'd love it," I said. I try not to make it a habit to answer for him, but I do it when I sense someone's impatience or a tendency to misunderstand. The cousin nodded and Marcel smiled, but in the remaining decade he lived in the nursing home, the cousin never found the time to stop by.

Today at camp, the first thing Marcel wants to do is show us the spot where he tent camps overnight. We roll out there with his housemate, Stephanie, and, at some point, they start racing. It's a slow race, but the ground is bumpy and uneven and it feels festive. They're both cracking up.

When the race is over, I tell Stephanie about the staff person who, last week when I was visiting, asked if I'm Marcel's mother. I'm forty-five. Marcel starts to laugh and Stephanie chortles. "Was it Jimmy?" she asks. He says yes. "Oh, God," she says. "Jimmy!" We all laugh.

Then Stephanie teases Steve about something and then we're back to making fun of me for spending so much on anti-wrinkle cream when it's clearly not working if someone thought I was the mother of a seventy-year-old man who, admittedly, looks pretty good, in part because he dyes his hair. We're all laughing so hard he's driving like a drunk, but it doesn't matter because the ground is flat and hard and there are no great ridges to fall off so he's fine.

I'm too young to be Marcel's mother, but Jimmy is not the first person to ask if I am. There's undeniably something maternal about our relationship. I feed him, wipe his nose when needed, and worry he's driving his chair too fast, too unsteadily, or that he isn't watching the road. No one ever thinks Steve is his father, even though he's older than I am.

Amy had Marcel's sixtieth party in the activity room of the nursing home, and I cancelled country singer Vicki Lee and the

VFW hall. Still, he was surprised by the party and happy to see family members he hadn't seen in years, all of whom lived within fifteen minutes of the nursing home. I thought that day would be a turning point. That his family would see how happy he was to see them and would want to visit, even just once in a while. They could come in pairs and talk to each other and let him be in the room with them and they would see his face break open with joy.

That day, among the chaos of kids running around his wheelchair and cousins asking after each other's parents, I offered to feed Marcel cake and Amy said that would be the easiest thing for her, seeing she was busy with everyone else. Amy reminded me to make sure I asked if he wanted the vanilla side or the chocolate side of the sheet cake she'd bought at the grocery store. I smiled. "Chocolate," I said. Maybe I was showing off a little, because I knew and she didn't know him at all. "If he picked vanilla over chocolate, I'd think he was dying," I said. She watched me, and so I asked him anyway. Marcel lowered his head, focused the laser affixed to his glasses, and typed out "chocolate." I had already cut the piece for him.

I helped him open cards from his family, most of which held ten or twenty dollars. I handed the cards and money to Amy, and then we don't know what happened. Marcel doesn't remember seeing the money again, but stealing birthday money seems like a terrible thing to accuse someone of.

Soon after his sixtieth birthday party, Amy stopped working at the nursing home and, other than by way of the occasional Facebook post, Marcel's never seen her again.

On his seventieth birthday, it takes us nearly an hour to walk down to the camp spot, but we're not in a hurry. It's secluded here—a wide clearing surrounded by trees with a little keyhole cutout down to the pond. We sit for a bit, take pictures, talk about how he likes to sleep outdoors and I do not. We look at the stone camp oven counselors use to make pizzas, the spot where the tents are anchored down, the sunlight on the water. I ask if they all tell ghost stories and Marcel says no and Stephanie says yes. I tell one I remember my dad telling me about a werewolf in the woods.

When Marcel's had enough at the camp spot, he rolls away. In the twenty-five years we've known each other, he's learned to trust that if he leaves, I will follow. He doesn't have to ask my permission. He usually checks in with me anyway, but I've already told him today is his day and whatever he wants goes. So, he leaves, and we follow.

On our way up to the treehouse, which has a ramp and wide doorways but is suspended just like any other tree house, he asks me to stop for a second.

We stop in the shade because in the sun, the laser on his glasses can't connect with his communication device. He's said before he doesn't understand how there's technology for TVs that work in the sun and are waterproof but not his communication device. Supply and demand, I tell him. Everyone has a TV, not many have a communication device.

Steve and Stephanie walk ahead to give us some privacy. He types in a question and I wait off to the side. I scroll through Facebook on my phone. I don't look over his shoulder and guess what he's going to ask, because that's like interrupting someone who stutters. It's been decades since he told me he doesn't like it when people read over his shoulder and I only do it now when I ask first and if I really can't understand what he said. Because he's never been to school, he spells only by sounding things out, and because the English language and the Maine accent are weird, sometimes his spelling is way off.

This time, he has his question prepared, so it only takes thirty seconds or so. I put my phone away. He asks if he should get in touch with Connie and Leta. I grimace and then try to make my face more neutral.

No, you shouldn't. That's what I want to say. I want to say they don't deserve his ongoing kindness. Where are they today, on his seventieth birthday? Did they send flowers or balloons or a singing gorilla? Did they call him or FaceTime him and sing Happy Birthday? Did they organize a car parade to go by his house and beep and wave? Did they leave him a cake on the doorstep or decorate the front of his door with streamers? Did they even send cards? No, they didn't. They posted messages on Facebook, which is their way of letting everyone know they care, except Marcel can't even check Facebook without my help, which I've told them before.

"If you want to," I say.

Connie met Marcel the same way he and I met, when he lived at the nursing home and she worked there. I was in Activities; Connie worked in Dietary. She and her family used to take him to hockey games, shopping, and over to their house. Then she got stomach cancer and, while she was in chemo and then recovering, she needed to stay away from germy places, which included nursing homes. But then she went into remission and changed jobs and she worked a lot of hours at her new job and her kids got older and—I don't know. She sometimes still sends cards that sit unopened in Marcel's backpack until he tells me they're there and I open and read them aloud. The cards always say how much she misses him.

What bothers me isn't that friendships sometimes run their course and maybe yours and Connie's falls into that category. What bothers me isn't the occasional card with updates on her health, her kids, her husband, her work. That's all fine. What bothers me is the repeated promise of trying to get together. Of saying you miss someone when, really, that could be rectified if it were true. If she really missed you, she'd stop by sometime. Or contact your house staff and arrange to meet you somewhere. The missing is, as far as I can tell, just a phrase Connie uses to close her letters and cards. Or maybe that's not fair. Maybe she misses the relationship you had but she knows that at this point in her life she can't commit to the amount of time or energy a friendship with you—or maybe anyone—requires. What she doesn't understand is that, to you, missing sounds like hope. What she doesn't understand is that you forgive her because you believe friendship with you is too much work.

I think friendships require different things at different times. Measuring it seems counterproductive.

Uncle Gil, who died maybe twenty years ago now, came to see Marcel a lot and really took over helping with paying bills and managing finances and doctor's appointments when Marcel's mom died in 1996. Whenever Gil saw us together, he teased that Marcel had a knack with the "pretty girls." He was a charmer, that Gil. Leta was his wife.

There are a lot of things you don't know about the interactions I've had with Leta over the years. The time I sent a group Facebook message to Leta and a few of your cousins asking for money to supplement the $30 a month you got from Medicaid when you lived in the nursing home and they accused me of stealing from you because they honestly couldn't understand what you would spend money on, seeing you had a roof over your head and three square meals a day. Going to the movies, I said. Sneakers, I said. Reese's peanut butter cups. They didn't believe me. Meet him at the grocery store and buy him a few snacks, I said, if you're worried about mishandling of funds. They said they would but they didn't.

Then there was the time you were in the hospital for two months and I practically begged Leta or one of your cousins to go see you, even just drop in, to lift your spirits and to give me a break and they refused because they said they don't know what to say to you. Say nothing,

I pleaded. Just be there. Read the newspaper. Just sit and watch TV. Just be a person in the room to remind the doctors that he's a person. There's a list of TV stations he likes to watch, I said. You could pop in, say hi, and put the TV on for him. Maybe, they said. But not one person in your family came to see you in all those months.

If I tell you the things your family has done or not done, you might see they're crappy human beings. Or you might think you don't deserve more than they're willing to give.

I don't think Marcel should waste his time reaching out to either Connie or Leta. But he's asking, which means it's been on his mind. I look at his sweet, earnest face and I say what a better version of me would say: "You should call them if you think that, on your deathbed, you'll regret not calling them." I'm almost patting myself on the back when I go ahead and add, "Even though they don't deserve it."

He nods at this.

We keep walking and catch up with Steve and Stephanie. I ask if I can tell Steve what we just talked about and he says I can. He says, "You're a good guy, Marcel." He rolls his eyes.

After a lunch of lobster rolls, orange soda, and the chocolate-peanut butter cake Marcel requested, we go for a ride on the boat. Marcel gestures for me to take the communication device off the wheelchair and then he gestures toward his lap belt. "Unbuckle you?"

"Yup," the counselor who looks too young to legally drive says. "All the straps."

This means Marcel's feet, too, which we never do because, even though he doesn't have seizures, his spasticity could make him slide right out of his chair. The counselor explains that if the boat sinks and he's strapped into his very heavy electric wheelchair, he will drown. "Ah," I say. Even though inside I panic a little to think I hadn't thought of that.

The boat doesn't sink. We're out on the calm, smooth, foliage-dotted lake for a solid hour. We see an eagle's nest and then, high up and startlingly white-headed, the eagle. Steve gets up, crosses to the front of the boat, and taps Marcel on the shoulder. Steve points so Marcel can follow his arm and see the eagle. Marcel smiles.

It's chilly but bright with sun. We are wind-blown and happy when we get back. We wrestle out of our life jackets and buckle Marcel back into his chair and I feel relief he's on solid ground.

The house staff who have waited in the van because they are from Rwanda and are freezing come out to give him his supplemental food through the feeding tube put in last year when Marcel lost more than sixty pounds and was in very real danger of dying. He decided to go ahead with the feeding tube, even though he didn't want one. He wanted to live more than he didn't want another surgery, another tube. There were a few bumps in the road, but it's fine now. He's gained weight. He feels good.

After Marcel gets food and then gets his ileostomy bag burped, he gestures with his head that he wants to go up a path I hadn't even noticed. "You lead, we'll follow," I say.

He takes us up to the athletic field, because that's where they have adaptable archery. In July when we came up to camp for the day, I said I wanted to try archery. We ran out of time that day, but Marcel never forgets anything. What I actually said was that he had to go out in the field and try to stay very still with an apple on his head. "It's a trust exercise," I said. He said Steve could go first. We all laughed. They said there would be no way they'd trust me aiming an arrow anywhere near their heads.

We just get to the field when it starts to rain and we joke that Marcel's off the hook with the whole apple-on-the-head thing. Steve lifts Marcel's communication device off his wheelchair and jogs back to the van. Usually, we keep a plastic bag handy so we can tie it over the computer in case it rains. But sometimes people clean out his backpack and so there's no bag in there today. Marcel and I roll back down the hill after Steve. There's no lightning, so I'm not worried about him in his metal chair. I could switch the chair to manual and run him back to the van, but he won't melt in a drizzle. And I don't really want to be done with this day. Marcel is seventy. He is happy. We walk and roll down the leaf-dotted path, my hand on his back. "I'm not going to start to cry again," I say. He laughs.

When Marcel is loaded back into the van and strapped in—one strap on each corner, an extra belt across his lap—I say, "Happy birthday."

"Thank you," he says. He says this with his breath, not his communication device. It's one of the clearest things he can say with his voice box, probably because it's the thing he says the most.

On the way home, Steve and I agree that we can't remember the last time we all laughed so much.

A week later, we meet up at Fort Williams in Cape Elizabeth for a walk. It's a beautiful day, full sun, and no shade anywhere so we can talk. That means I can only ask you yes or no questions. We roll down a huge grassy hill, me a nervous wreck, Steve with his hands on your chair only because I insist he have them there in case you start going too fast.

"Have you thought any more about calling Connie and Leta?" I ask.

You nod.

"Have you called yet?"

You shake your head no.

We walk down a path near the water. It's narrow, and I keep nudging you away from the cliff. When we get to the wider section with a fence in front of us and, beyond that Portland Head Light and the ocean, I ask, "Are you going to call?"

You stare at me.

I venture, "Not sure?"

You nod.

You roll toward the truck selling iced coffee and you gesture with your head and I understand you want one. I add in the five creams and five sugars you take. I fish out a flexible straw from the supply we keep in your backpack and hold the cup and straw so you can drink, then resume our conversation. "That's okay," I say. "You can take your time. They've taken their time."

A couple of weeks after that, we meet for another walk. You head into the shade and ask if I'll help you write an email to Leta.

"Today?" I ask. We only have an hour and a half here, and I think we both want to be in the sun.

"No," you say. "Sometime."

I touch your back. "Of course I will."

For Marcel's seventy-fourth birthday, we actually manage to pull off a surprise. We rent the function room at a bowling alley, invite Marcel's friends, and buy orange balloons and a chocolate cake with chocolate icing.

He knows something's going on when he comes in and Steve steers him away from the bowling lanes and toward the closed doors of a room. He starts to laugh when I open the doors and we all yell "Surprise! Happy Birthday!"

And then he looks at me, and looks at everyone gathered, and I see genuine surprise and delight on his face.

His case worker, who has known him longer than I have, his one-time nurse and her granddaughters, his friends from church, his housemates, my friend's eleven-year-old son who has cerebral palsy and has become friends with Marcel, his friend from camp, his favorite house staff, us.

There's no family here, not the biological kind, but there's the family he's created in the seventy-four years of his life, the people who love him and love being around him.

And that's the point of all of this.

Epilogue

I wanted Marcel's voice to be the place where this book landed, so I asked him to write something about why he wanted me to write his story and what he wanted people to get from it. At first, he resisted, shaking his head at me before I'd even finished asking. He worried, as always, that he wouldn't be able to say exactly what he wanted to say. I told him by now, at the end of this book, people will have come to love him as much as I do. He nodded and then, occasionally stopping to look up in thought, typed a message on his communication device.

> I AM MARCEL LEMELIN I WHY I DID WRITE THIS BOOK FOR TELL WHO I AM AND GET THE PEOPLE TO KNOW ME AND UNDERSTAND ME.

SOURCES

Downnar, James, Tracy Luk, Robert W. Sibbald, Tatiana Santini, Joseph Mikhael, Hershl Berman, and Laura Hawryluck. "Why Do Patients Agree to a 'Do Not Resuscitate' or 'Full Code' Order? Perspectives of Medical Inpatients." *Journal of General Internal Medicine* 26, no. 6 (June 2011): 582-87.

Fitzsimons, Nancy. "For Minnesota's Disabled Adults, Freedom To Be Intimate Is Rare." *Star Tribune* (Minneapolis), November 12, 2015.

Johnson, Emily. "Disability, Medicine, and Ethics." *AMA Journal of Ethics* (April 2016)

Maine Human Rights Act, Title 5, §4630, "Discrimination by public entities prohibited," Maine Legislature, https://www.mainelegislature.org/legis/statutes/5/title5sec4630.html

National Disability Navigator Resource Collaborative, https://nationaldisabilitynavigator.org/

National Health Law Program. "Maine Nursing Home Residents with Disabilities Celebrate Long Awaited Move to the Community." November 15, 2013. https://healthlaw.org/news/mainenursing-home/

"Out of the Shadows: The Legacy of Pineland," https://shadowsofpineland.org

Reichman, Nancy E., Hope Corman, and Kelly Noonan. "Impact of Child Disability on the Family." *Maternal and Child Health Journal* 12, no. 6 (November 2008): 679-83.

Thornberry, Catherine, and Karin Olson. "The Abuse of Individuals with Developmental Disabilities." *Developmental Disabilities Bulletin* 33, nos. 1-2 (2005): 1-19.

Thomson, Rosemarie Garland. "Seeing the Disabled: Visual Rhetorics of Disability in Popular Photography." In *New Disability History: Amer-*

ican Perspectives, edited by Paul K. Longmore and Lauri Umansky. New York: New York University Press, 2001.

Trishla Foundation, "Cerebral Palsy Life Expectancy," https://www.trishlafoundation.com/cerebral-palsy-life-expectancy/

ABOUT THE AUTHOR

SARAH COPPERBURG

Jen Dupree is the author of two novels, *The Miraculous Flight of Owen Leach* (2022) and *What Do You Want from Me?* (2025). She is an assistant editor for *The Masters Review*, a library director, and a former bookstore owner. She has an MFA in Creative Writing from the University of Southern Maine's Stonecoast program. Her work has appeared in *December*, *Solstice*, *The Masters Review*, *On the Rusk,* and other notable places. She is the winner of the *Writer's Digest* Fiction Contest for 2017 and a two-time winner of a Maine Literary Award (2006, 2022). She lives in Maine with her husband and Portuguese water dog (Pink) Floyd. Find her at www.JenniferDupree.com.

ACKNOWLEDGMENTS

This book would not exist without the encouragement and support of many people. Most especially Dr. Garber, my therapist, who first suggested I write about Marcel and who patiently listened as I explained every reason why I couldn't. To Melanie Brooks, Elisha Emerson, and Jess Pulver, my deep gratitude for their many thoughtful readings of these pages. To KJ Grow and the entire team at Islandport Press, sincere thanks for seeing what I saw in this book and helping to make it so much more than I could have hoped. Thanks also to Rochelle Bourgault for her careful, compassionate reading and gentle reshaping of my words. To my husband, Steve, who is my first reader and the best human I know, thank you for loving Marcel as much as I do and for being so good to both of us. And to you, Marcel, without whose joy and enthusiasm this book would not exist. Thank you for trusting me to write this. Your friendship is one of my life's greatest gifts.